Heroine Tales

So no woman has to slay her dragons alone

ISBNs
Paperback: 978-1-64184-490-1
Ebook: 978-1-64184-491-8

Table of Contents

~

Introduction

Once upon a time, in a land far, far away, lived two princesses. They resided in separate castles, had separate parents, and lived separate lives. When their paths eventually crossed, they knew, they just knew, that within each other, they had found a soul sister.

Before they came together, their journeys were not always easy; in fact, they were sometimes harsh and even dark. At times, they felt like they were facing dragons from fairy tales. And even after coming into each other's lives, they still encountered their dragons except now, they had the love and support of a soul sister to witness their tribulations, turnarounds, and triumphs.

Within each princess came the desire to share her story and invite other princesses to do the same. Women's stories deserve to be told and should not be hidden away in an ivory tower. When we are willing to speak the real and raw truth of our struggles with authenticity and honesty, and when we share how we went from being a damsel in distress to our own knights in shining armor, we help other princesses realize that they do not have to slay their dragons alone. They do not need to be rescued, and within them lies great power. Because we are, in fact, not only princesses, but also the Heroines of our own tales.

Thank you for taking the journey into our "Heroine Tales." May you find your story in these tales and be inspired and empowered to become the Heroine you already are.

Michelle Davis
Michele Whittington

Stories

Who Am I?

By Anonymous

As I sat in the aisle seat ready to take off on my first-ever airplane flight, I tried several times unsuccessfully to make the buckle meet the other end of the seatbelt. A flight attendant walking by said to me quietly, "Oh, let me get you a seatbelt extender." A few minutes later, a different flight attendant stood in the center aisle holding the extender aloft and loudly asked, "Who needs the seat belt extender?" I was only 23 years old at the time, but for the entirety of my now 60+ years, the "seat belt extender" was a metaphor for my life - always trying to make myself fit in, instead of being who I AM.

I was a very large baby. Once I tasted food for the first time, it became a love affair that resulted in morbid obesity for the next 60 years. I vividly remember being weighed in front of my 4th-grade classmates and the look on the nurse's face when she saw that I weighed 99 pounds. That year, my classmates gave me the nickname *Sub*, short for submarine, and that is when I learned that self-deprecating humor made it hurt much less.

I reached 200 pounds by the time I entered high school and already started to develop many of the physical ailments associated with morbid obesity - prediabetes, sleep apnea, arthritic joints, shortness of breath, and congestive heart failure. By the time I graduated from college, I was well on my way to the 300-pound mark. Physically, I was a mess, but emotionally, I was an even bigger mess.

Everything about me has been shaped by my history of morbid obesity. I have been shy and introverted my entire life, trying to fit my 300-pound body into spaces designed for much smaller people who often judged me because of my size. If I could not fit, I would hide and try not to be seen. It took a toll on my self-esteem. I had great self-confidence in my intellectual capabilities. However, I felt like a failure because I was too ashamed to put myself out there and embrace my intellect and talents. I had an incredibly low opinion of myself and seriously doubted my worthiness to be alive.

In 2002, I lost a very dear friend due to heart complications resulting from morbid obesity. She was my age. Rather than using her death as a motivation to make myself healthier, I secretly hoped the same thing could happen to me. Fortunately, things started to change for me in 2005, when I met my first and, to date, only love. Caring about her made me care more about myself. I met a whole new set of friends through her and developed a loving support system.

I began living a healthier lifestyle and taking better care of myself. I started to lose some of my weight and gained some self-confidence. I was happier than I had ever been. Then, unexpectedly in 2012, she passed away from a very rare and fatal disease. My move out of state to be with her now left me feeling alone and isolated. Her death pushed me into a downward spiral, during which I regained all of the weight I had lost, plus another 50 pounds.

I moved back to my home state and started a long and isolated period of all work and no play. I was a crazy cat woman with 2 cats that were my only reason for being. My love for them and their total dependence on me was what kept me going. Day by day, I ignored the friends who had become my support system and threw myself into my job.

Even though I abandoned my friends, my friends never abandoned me. One of them encouraged me to come to church with her. I was never much of a church person, having grown up with an atheist father. My girlfriend had been a church music director before she passed away, and I had attended with her, but I was more interested in the music and the fellowship than the message. I lacked any understanding of God and spirituality.

Looking back, I can now see that this church invitation was the major turning point for where I am today. Something was starting to bubble up in me. I started to enjoy the minister's message and began to explore the idea that I am perfect just because I AM. I only have to be me, and I don't have to live up to anyone else's expectations about who I should be.

I decided to volunteer at the church, and it felt good to do something worthwhile for a change.

One of the church's young staff members seemed very aloof toward me, as was I to her. My perception was that she did not like me, and we could not connect. However, over the next couple of years, there was a noticeable transformation in her. She had worked on becoming healthier, seemed to develop a new sense of self-confidence, and exuded warmth and friendliness as well as a new glow from within. I began to admire her strength to make positive changes.

Her transformation motivated me to want to do the same. If she could do it, I could do it. I had recently seen my doctor, and she had told me it was time to choose - focus on getting healthy or likely risk an early death. It seemed like the right time to decide to change. In 2017, I gave myself the gift of Bariatric weight loss surgery. There were many hoops to jump through for insurance and many protocols designed to help ensure lasting success. It took several months of medical office visits, tests, psychological counseling, group support meetings, dietary changes, and exercise classes, before I could have the surgery. It was not the "easy way out," as many people think.

I started attending exercise classes 8 months before my surgery. In the beginning, I was gasping for air after 2-3 minutes on a very slow treadmill, and every muscle and joint in my body hurt. I hated every minute of it, but I persevered and developed the exercise habit. Now, I enjoy the high that exercise gives me. Sometimes, I am too tired or don't want to take the time to exercise, and I don't always enjoy it in the moment, but the high after a good workout is worth it.

The surgery, exercise, and dietary changes enabled me to lose 160 pounds and eliminated many of the medical conditions that were debilitating me. Consequently, I did gain some self-confidence. I am no longer as self-conscious about the size of my body. I would consider sitting in the middle airplane seat if necessary, and I no longer panic at the thought of wearing a swimsuit in public. Clothes shopping has become much more comfortable though I am overwhelmed by the selection and variety, and I still haven't discovered my "style."

Changing my outer world was the easy part. The hard part has been changing my inner world. The physical act of losing weight has been much less difficult than the mental and emotional aspects that go along with it. I am still shy and insecure about my self-worth. I have realized that I need to work on more than the size of my body by redefining who I believe I am and how I want to show up in the world.

I was recently participating in a self-growth class when one of the participants described her avocation as helping people "become and feel beautiful." This piqued my interest because I had never considered myself beautiful and wondered if I could ever "become" so. I started to think about what it meant to be beautiful. Beauty is in the eye of the beholder, but to my mind, few people have inherent physical beauty. For most of us, beauty has to come from an inner glow that shows up in our presentation of ourselves to others - the way we smile, make eye contact, carry ourselves, interact, etc. It can be aided by externals such as clothing, hair, and makeup, but it has to originate from how we honestly feel about ourselves and how we project that to others.

I am not sure that I will ever be able to convince myself that I have inherent physical beauty. I know I have to work on how I feel about and value myself in order to be beautiful. I think of it as a reverse of the Golden Rule; do unto myself as I would do unto others. I have been aided in this by connecting with groups of other like-minded women who have loved and supported me to reach my highest potential. In return, I have been blessed to support them in the same way.

This journey of self-discovery has been full of potholes, U-turns, and bends in the road. However, with a lot of help from my friends, teachers, and mentors, I am choosing to stay on the path to grow my self-esteem, acknowledge the real me, and project my inner beauty regardless of my body's shape and size, simply because I AM.

Or Was It?

By Carla B

The 8-year-old me stepped into the elementary classroom that morning acutely aware of the small size of the room even though my short stature normally made the room feel large. Homemade Christmas decorations were placed all about the room. The wicked things that had occurred to me at the hand of my father earlier that morning stung at my soul and physical body. As the day progressed, I was somehow able to navigate the classroom and my feelings. I even navigated interactions with adults just as if the last 8 hours had not been wrought with suffocating confusion and pain.

The memory and details of the first time I experienced incest would eventually fade into a type of murky cave in my mind. If you have ever been in an underground cave, you may have an idea of how this felt. This cave is where the memory of each ugly experience would go to reside; it's where the dragon lived. The incest would continue for nearly 3 years until the end of

4th grade. It happened intermittently, but most often in the soft hours of 6-7 am.

Throughout my teen and early adult years, I would recall the design on some of the sheets and the feel of his rough hand lightly yet firmly against my mouth. Each time the incest occurred, I was aware that I added a layer to an emotional and mental shell to protect me from this reality. I was young; the reality was harsh. The armor around my heart and mind would protect me. I knew this with great and determined certainty.

This protection of layers I built would become a superpower of sorts. Yes, a superpower. I was polished, gracious, funny, and articulate at a young age. In school, my teachers would praise me for my poise and ability to speak in front of crowds. The superpower allowed me to shine and be externally, at times, authentically happy. My body would respond with an attitude and determination of, "I will show them (him)."

At the age of 16, I experienced a loving and passionate sexual experience with my high school sweetheart. His love and sweetness of spirit were all I would need for the rest of my life. However, the shell I had created and the dragon that haunted my heart would not allow that to be my future. Wasted blocks of time of jealousy and anxious behavior coupled with an underlying desire to flirt and tempt promiscuousness led to the demise of what should have been a story of life-long love.

Upon entry into college, I moved boldly (brightly on the outside) into my new independent world. I chose to use men to demonstrate my edgy intelligence and power. Even while in a committed relationship, I would objectify a man and make certain to leave his heart knowing (in my mind) who was in charge. I entered my 30s selecting men with whom to have sex for the sole reason to let them know clearly, usually around 4 am, *that it was time for him to leave now.*

Let's remember my superpower; I was fun, dazzling, spirited, a good friend, and a fabulous employee. It was all working out fine, or was it?

In my late 30s, I met a man who was kind, very basic, very normal, supported by a kind family, and full of integrity. He admired me, my mind, my body, and my humor. About a year into this relationship, I found out that I was pregnant. I was so in love with the life growing inside of me that I shared my news with 2 of my best friends. In that moment, I felt a cracking of my superpower shell; it felt like a hard-boiled egg being tapped on the counter. The superpower didn't subside, but its exterior was now fractured.

It was plainly evident that the best thing to do was to get married and settle down. Motherhood suited me. I was radiant and loving, and all was good, or was it? My shell's superpower was about the flash, the action, the words, the laughs, and the control, and unfortunately, it did not include settling down into a domestic routine. Beneath the profound love that I felt for the tiny girl in my belly was shame, hurt, and a growing anger. As always, the superpower allowed me to remain poised and calm, always offering the best anecdotes, confidence, and stellar ideas at work.

It wasn't until after the birth of my second baby girl that the torment of my past seemed to rise to a rapid boil within me. As many memories emerged from the cave, there was now a struggle of sorts, including mental, emotional, and even physical challenges. There was a yearning of my soul to break out and away from that shell and face the memories. *Why would I do that?* The shell protecting me from the dragon in the cave was a public mask that kept me from suffering, or was it?

I loved, and still love, my daughters with a depth and complex beauty few can understand. My superpower allowed for this unique love. I nurtured and loved from a unique angle and perspective. There was the occasional screaming at my daughters; there was the occasional break down in my health and moments of indiscretion, which would at times impede progress at work, but the superpower allowed me to expand and rise, so it was fine, or was it?

As my daughters began school, my shell began to weaken even more because specific memories from those tender years began to take solid hold in my mind. I would take extended time frames away from my daughters because I didn't want to "poison" them with my emotional outbursts and sadness. I found that when you love profoundly, you cannot hide the reality of the heart.

During this time, I traveled the world for work and found a special and handsome lover, but the relationship was short-lived, of course. Plus, he cheated on me. However, I was pleasantly living above my pain. The dragon in the cave from my youth was pushed aside and down; it was working perfectly, or was it? I would rationalize to myself, while sitting on a plane or sleeping in a hotel room, that my superpower was going to protect me and cover the pain of the past, or was it?

The shell itself was falling away just like that hard-boiled eggshell, a small piece here and a large piece there. The superpower itself was muscle memory, but the shell was leaving me. Like watching a movie, I would observe myself crying and driving way too fast, drinking too much alcohol, and spending too much money. It appeared that this combination was what I needed to assuage and satisfy my hurt and feed my superpower, or was it?

Something else I experienced throughout my 20s, 30s, and 40s was the disturbing issue that I was never comfortable in a dentist's chair. It was the position, a man's hand near my mouth; it was terrifying for me. I recall going to a dentist in Bethesda, MD, thinking I was able to rise above the issues. I began crying as soon as they put the blue paper bib on me. I left. I can almost see the dentist and assistant's face to this day. I walked home and cried myself to sleep.

I was smart, had a lucrative job, and good health insurance. On several occasions in my early 30s, I attempted counseling and therapy. These attempts at counseling and therapy would lead to some type of unusual friendship with the provider/therapist. I possessed a skill of spinning the story and sharing the pain that turned into some type of (sick?) entertainment for the therapist sitting in the chair across from me. The professionals would somehow assure me that I had my emotions and forward path under control. My friends, however, I did not.

Thus far, we have my backstory and a glimpse into some moments of adulthood. It's time that I share the "slaying of the dragon." It's time I share with you how I forgave, expanded, learned to love myself, and finally broke the shell. The dragon was ready to be slayed.

I was in my early 40s, and I was ready to actually live AND, most importantly, no longer let the bitter taste of my life influence my daughters. I did not want the residue and overspill from my pain to seep into their beliefs and/or fears. It was time for the removal of the shell and the use of my superpower from the inside out that would accomplish this most meaningful goal.

On a particularly beautiful Sunday in June, my oldest daughter and I attended a church service. The Senior Minister, a beautiful soul who could touch each heart with ease and directness, was speaking that day. Her words focused on stepping into your highest and best self and how to use the stories (even the ugly ones) from the past to create the best future. If only I had a transcript to share; the words cut like razor blades to my emotional heart. They were cuts, like from a surgery, that were required for one to live.

After leaving the church, I had a frank (buckets of tears) conversation with my daughter as she drove the car. I was far too emotional to drive. Her 15½-year-old self was thrilled she was driving, and I could feel the juxtaposition occurring as her heart had to hear my story. I told her my story because I needed her to know that if anything (past or future) is painful that it is necessary to face it, to work with it, and not to allow that story to impose or dilute the beauty and success that is hers to have. She expressed that she was proud of me, learned from my story, and deeply loved me. Her love saturated the interior of the car and my total being. A new superpower began to overtake my emotions and soul - a true superpower!

After that day and time with my daughter, I began to make huge strides toward my own internal healing. The reality is that I had to slay that dragon to build and expand. I connected daily with spiritual practices, including mantra chanting, meditation, drumming, yoga, and breathwork. Overall, I began to organize my life to include spiritual practices and spiritual people. Those ritual practices became, and still remain, a predominant part of my daily life.

I also made a promise to myself to no longer be promiscuous because of my dragon. I began to fully honor myself when in a committed relationship. If the other person did not honor themselves (if they cheated), I stirred up strength and continued forward with an open heart. I'm stunningly proud to say I've kept this promise to myself! It is a journey brought about by the slaying of the dragon.

I also had made a promise to myself to go to the dentist and overcome that fear. The angel of that year, the hero in my own superpower story, was a gracious and spiritual dentist with whom I was able to share my story. What a day that was! He worked carefully and kindly and eventually fitted me with braces. The braces allowed me to eliminate physical evidence of my father's DNA influence, an overlapped front tooth. I now have my own bright smile.

I may choose to write a longer "how-to" regarding my years of work to keep all the pieces of the shell away and to retain the superpower. But for now, I want to share with you a few of the ways in which I *know* that my journey and my work indeed slayed my dragons! They include meditation, chanting, exercise, laughter, clearing away toxic people, and finding the REAL me inside of me. I worked slowly and diligently at allowing a pure, true light to shine from within. The superpower is brightly present, but with a monumental difference. The superpower now comes from inside the heart, not from that external shell created when I was 8. That shell is gone.

My youngest daughter comments on the "new and improved Mom." Due to my internal work, she was inspired to create her own "clean slate" after making some less than favorable choices in her late teen years. She's bold, determined, and strong, and I am proud of her! My oldest daughter is thriving and has a spirit that cannot be dimmed. She likes to tease her father and me by saying, "Why did you two raise me so good? I know what I want, and I know that I can get it!" These two girls are amazing. I am amazing. Our superpowers are coming from the inside out.

From the earliest moment the shell started to crack, I attracted some special individuals, <u>deep and long-lasting friends</u>. Previously, I had not had deep friendships as I had always been *on-the-move*. These friends are spiritual, fun, funny, wicked smart, and always offer unconditional love. I became a member of a tribe; in fact, I created a tribe! Some of these tribe members knew parts of my story; some did not. The beauty is that I attracted people who honored me right where I was, and I honored them right where they were. These tribe members are in it for the long run. I believe some use the term "ride or die" friends. I feel inclined to share their initials; RDG, JB, RE, LMc, PA, LM, RD, MD, and MW. As soon as *you* begin to slay your dragon, find your tribe and love, love them!

Health and vitality are blessed benefits of slaying the dragon. My body now has a desire to move, to be involved, to try new activities, and overall, to be healthy. As the years have progressed, I have found healthy living, a healthy diet, and a variety of exercises allow my light to shine via love and not via control. Here's to health!

Dragons are real in your stories and in mine. They hurt and they sting. However, within us is the light, the magic potion to slay our dragons. The light inside of me (and I see it in you too) guided me to a place where everything was fine, or was it? The answer is, finally, "Yes!"

YES! A resounding, slain dragon, lovely daughters, loving relationship filled YES!

It was <u>and is</u> a steady, sweet, tough, tear-filled, and peaceful working and evolving journey. The lessons will come from surprising places. For me, healing came through chanting mantras, that special dentist, and a new (and the best) romantic relationship. You will cry, and you will work, and you will slay that dragon! Much love — Me.

The Mountains I've Climbed

By Tara Brown

A aron yelled, "Tara, look at me, stay awake! Stay with me!"
I was lying in a pool of blood, having just been thrown
sideways onto the ground after a failed turn on my mountain
bike. My head had hit a rock that sliced my forehead just under
my helmet. I could feel the warm blood on my face and hair. I
looked at my left arm, and it was no longer straight. Apparently,
it was a gruesome sight.

"Lucas," Aaron yelled again, "call 911!"

My head will mend quickly, I thought. I heard the thump when
I landed, no loss of consciousness. It was my arm, my darned arm,
that would keep me off of my bike for the next several months.
Damn. We were only 50 feet away from the trailhead.

I was exhausted after a 3½-hour-long, 27.5-mile ride, with
3,200 feet of elevation gain in 90-degree heat and full Arizona

sun. We were heading off of the single track to ride the canals back to our cars. It was a simple turn, from single-track to a wide gravel path. A 4-year old could have made that turn, but my bike slipped out from under me and threw me hard and fast into the ground. Thump. My left arm braced the fall, probably saving my skull from being fractured. My head hit a rock.

I was training for the Whiskey 30 Proof Mountain Bike Race, which is held in late April in Prescott, Arizona, and was only 2 months away. *Could I still ride in it? Could I heal in time?* Lying there on the ground, a wave of calm washed over me. Somehow, I knew that this would bring me forward and move me closer to my dream.

This belied the utter exhaustion I'd felt a little while earlier, while riding with a lost contact, walking my bike up trail sections I normally could ride through. A part of me had thought I was crazy. What was a 53-year-old woman doing training for the first time for a legendary mountain bike race? It all started 6 years earlier; I'd had a dream to be able to run a 5k in less than 30 minutes. What, you might ask, does that have to do with mountain biking?

Everything.

Steve Jobs said, "You can't connect the dots looking forward; you can only connect them looking backward."

****

It was 3 o'clock in the morning, and I couldn't sleep again. My stomach was sick, tied in knots. I had just filed for divorce, ending a long-term marriage that had become unhealthy. I had loved my husband. However, he made it clear that he didn't care about me anymore.

"I will pay for you and the kids to live here, and I'm getting my emotional and physical needs met elsewhere," he said.

Three am, night after night, I'd awaken in terror. I was unsure how I'd make a living; the economy was still in the great recession. As an architect with lapsed skills and a cold network, I had no idea how I'd make it. I hadn't worked for nearly 7 years. The only clear idea I had was something I'd kept as Plan B. I needed a positive place to park my mind, so I leveraged the last money I had as a down payment and became certified as a life coach.

Following that practice, I created a vision for my new life. That early vision included imagining what a healthy version of me would be able to do. Run a 5k in less than 30 minutes became the goal, yet, I wouldn't start working on it for 4 more years. In those years, I rebuilt my career, bought a house, and made new friends. I learned to navigate life on my own.

That was a significant goal for me. In my late 20s, I had Epstein Barr Syndrome, and if I exercised for a half-hour, I'd need to sleep for 2 hours or more to recover. By the age of 34, I weighed over 220 pounds on my 5' 6" frame. I was the fat wife; I endured humiliation. That year, when I discussed with my then-husband my desire to have kids, he told me that I needed to get thin, find a job I liked, and make myself happy in the next 6 months or he'd divorce me.

Believing it was all my fault, I did everything I could to change myself into the woman he wanted. I hired a trainer, joined a 12-step program, dieted, and got therapy. It worked, and I released 60 pounds, keeping it off until I became pregnant with twins. I remember reading in the books that a twins' mom should gain 55-60 pounds with a healthy pregnancy. You can imagine how much that messed with my head, as I'd worked so hard to release that much weight.

Yet, I followed the doctor's orders, gained the weight, visualized surrendering my pregnant uterus to God, drank a gallon of water a day, and Gave birth to 2 healthy girls via scheduled C-Section. Doctors and nurses congratulated me on their size and health. Life looked perfect. Then the pressure started.

Six weeks after delivery, he'd say, "When are we having sex?" "When are you going to get birth control?" "What's wrong with you?" "Many women would think I'm a catch!" "All I'd have to do is go to a bar and wave a few $100 bills, and I could have any woman I wanted." "Did you know prostitution is legal in Singapore?" "Did you know it only costs $100 for a prostitute?"

He had a calendar. He'd keep track of the days of the week when we had sex or not. If the numbers were fewer than twice a week, even for a nursing mom of twin newborns, I was in trouble. He'd shame me, humiliate me. He'd tell me that I was broken, and if I were *fixed*, our marriage would work.

It was awful. I felt awful. We stayed married for 7 more years. It nearly cost me my life.

The first dream I created was a dream of a healthy running body, wonderful relationships, meaningful work, and a sense of freedom. This dream seemed so far away, nearly impossible, even as a target 3 years into the future. Yet, I did what I could, baby steps. I revamped my resume. I had informational interviews with friends over lunch. I found a job.

I'd later realize that I was rebuilding my life from ashes; I was becoming a human Phoenix.

During the divorce, in an effort to support my health, I saw a Naturopathic doctor. She did a thorough analysis and helped me with supplements, bloodwork, and regular checkups. We became a team to help me stay healthy. At the end of 2017, we were at a routine checkup when she said, "Let's look at your blood work from 3 years ago."

Three years is a magic number to me; it's the number of years out that I work with myself and my clients on designing a life they'd love. It's just far enough away that our belief system thinks it might be possible to have new results.

She said, "Three years ago, this hormone was 0; we couldn't even find a trace of it in your system."

I said, "I knew that if I'd have stayed in that marriage, I'd be sick."

She looked at me, went silent for what felt like a long time, and said, "No, you'd be dead."

That sunk in. No, I'd be dead. I realized then what she'd known for 3 years and had kept to herself. It took that 3 years to rebuild the foundation of my life, and I chose to focus on my health. If I wanted to attract a healthy relationship where he and I lived an active life together, I needed to be the matching partner. I realized it was time to start working on that 5k.

I'd get up at 5:30 am and run while the kids were sleeping so I could get home before they woke up. At first, it was dark outside, and I wore a headlamp. I'd run 3 minutes, walk 1 minute, for a mile, then 2. Eventually, I worked my way up to 3 slow miles.

One day, midsummer, I was running my slow intervals while my mind explored the idea of orgasmic gratitude. Orgasmic gratitude is gratitude that feels so good that its closest kin is the feeling of an orgasm, like when you take a bite of delicious food that tastes absolutely perfect. Breathing hard, hot sun at my back, I wondered what would happen if I could experience orgasmic gratitude while running? Could I find this good feeling despite the burning in my legs and lungs? I asked my body to allow for orgasmic gratitude to flow through me, and something shifted. The 4-minute intervals didn't hurt as much.

In only 6 weeks, I progressed from running/walking for 45 minutes and suffering to trail running/walking for an hour and a half and feeling great afterward. It was a big celebratory day for me when I could run from my house to the trailhead, run the 3.1-mile trail loop, and run home! That goal had been established when I bought my house back in 2015.

A girlfriend suggested that I try running the Ragnar Trail, McDowell Mountain. At first, I couldn't imagine being strong enough to do 15.4 miles in a 24-hour relay race, but when I looked at the training schedule for new racers, I realized I was exactly on target. We signed up.

I remember panting and cursing as I ran the 4.7-mile leg on the competitive mountain bike track in the desert; my lights illuminated the dark trail, the chilly starry night, and me going up and down, up and down, on these small quick hills. I thought the 6.7-mile leg was supposed to be the hardest, yet this one had as much elevation gain and hurt way more.

I chanted a mantra, "This would be so fun on a mountain bike," over and over on the endless seeming knolls, not knowing how prescient that statement would be. My pace times were 12 - 12:30 minutes a mile, and I was pleased. I wasn't close to my less than 10 minutes a mile goal; however, it was tremendous progress. This race showed me how much I like the race scene, which included people of all sizes and shapes out to better themselves and cheer on their friends and teammates. I wanted more.

Adding more days to my running schedule each week didn't seem friendly to my body; I was still heavy at nearly 180 lbs., and so I thought about trying a triathlon. I found a sprint-distance triathlon on St. Patrick's Day, 2019. I was turning 52 at the end of the month, and this would be a celebration. It was also a "fuck you" of sorts to my Ex, who had done several triathlons with his sister, all while I felt terribly left out.

That little decision, to attempt a short triathlon, to try something new, unlocked my life.

The day after Christmas, I'd end up injured and couldn't run for the next 2 months. I bought a bike and did a little riding. I'd been a strong swimmer in my youth and did some practice laps in the pool. My right hip muscles unlocked enough to allow me to run again a few weeks before the race. I felt neither ready nor strong, but I showed up on race day anyway.

Races are grouped by categories, and in mine, I came in just out of the top 25% for men and women overall. That felt good. When I looked more closely at the results, I came in fourth fastest on the bike in my class for both men and women. I was stunned.

My entire life, I thought other people were athletes, my Ex, guys I'd dated, friends, but not me. I was mercilessly teased as the fat kid. I was the fat wife. I'd had Epstein-Barr. I never saw myself as an athlete and certainly not a cyclist. I realized in that moment - I had a capacity for cycling that I hadn't tapped into yet.

I wondered if I could do this, and what would happen if I tried? The next question became *do I focus on road or mountain biking?* Mountain biking was something I'd done off and on, never well, but it felt like 12-year-old-kid fun, and it scared me. The coaching work had taught me that the things that scare me would make me grow. I chose mountain biking.

Talking to a close friend, she challenged me when I told her that I wanted to get reasonably good at mountain biking.

"Enter a race," she said.

"Damn you," I said, grinning. She was right.

If I were to enter a race, I asked myself *what I would do?* Well, I'd need to get riding skills, hire a trainer, and get fit. I'd need to find people to ride with. I made a Facebook post, "I'm tired of being a chicken shit beginner; I want to become reasonably good at mountain biking." I connected with a group of guys, now my riding brothers, who helped me. They rode with me when I was painfully slow, walking up the slightest incline, riding fast at 7.8 miles an hour.

My skills coach suggested a race, Dawn2Dusk, and I signed up with my guys. The team that rides the most 16-mile laps in 12 hours wins. We wouldn't be the fastest, but we had a goal of at least 9 laps. I had 6 months to get in shape and learn to ride.

I'd get up at 5 am to go to the gym and workout, get home by 6:30 to get the kids up and ready for school and get me ready for work. Some days, I worked out twice. I rode my mountain bike Saturdays and Sundays. Slowly, I built up the miles, 10, 12, 15, eventually 20-mile rides. I had a goal; I wanted to do my laps averaging 12 miles an hour or faster. My best time had been 9.8 miles an hour. Twelve miles per hour was a significant increase.

My trainer had me working out at the threshold of over-working. I was tired a lot and exhilarated. My riding brothers, it turned out, liked to race. So, by the time our D2D race came about, I'd already been in 4 races. One was a 50-mile road ride that ended up with me being hospitalized 2 weeks later, 1 week before the D2D race, with an abscess on my sitz bone.

The ER doctors and nurses looked at me pitifully as I lay on the gurney, telling them I had a bike race in a week. The chief Resident, a tiny and powerful woman, said, "I have a friend like you. He's a triathlete; he doesn't listen to me either. I won't give you permission."

"If I ride, will I injure myself?" I asked.

"No, but it will hurt like a deep bruise," she said.

I could handle the pain. I'd had a twin pregnancy after all. Doing what I could do, riding a recumbent bike, lifting the weights I could lift, soaking my bottom 4 times a day in a sitz bath as prescribed, I rode in that race. My 2 lap times were faster than 12 mph. Not only had I achieved my goal, but I did it despite a lifetime of reasons why I couldn't.

I had become an athlete.

The New Paradigm of Healing

By Joyce Blair Buekers

"Music is the universal language of all cultures—so is Love."

Let me tell you a story of how the harp saved my life, and how the heart and the brain, when we take a moment to PAUSE, can change our lives. My passion is a whole new paradigm of healing that changes how we treat people dealing with countless challenges, such as opioid addiction and depression and the impact of the journey I took to get to this place of understanding.

You see, the energy, resonance, and frequencies of harp music connect with your heart and brain in ways that not only soothe, but also promote physical, emotional, mental, relational, and spiritual healing. I never realized what a powerful, scientifically proven healing instrument the harp would prove to be. The magic of the harp is what saved my life.

I grew up in an artistic family of musicians on my mother's side; science and technology on my father's side. My grandmother was a world-renowned harpist and the first woman in the Los Angeles Philharmonic who went on to play for Disney Studios for 40 years. She was the harpist for the movie *Fantasia*. She inspired my mother, my sisters, my daughter, and me to follow in her footsteps.

I thought about becoming a professional harpist at one point, but my father's advice about the computer field won me over at the time. He was the Branch Manager for Computer Timesharing with General Electric here in Phoenix in the 60s and convinced me that it was much more lucrative to pioneer in the computer field. I was hired as the first woman in the Phoenix division of IBM Data Processing in the mid-70s.

My story of discovery begins with a horrific life-changing tragedy. As you may already know, many events in life, in retrospect, are major blessings. After 15 years with IBM, I was a recipient of an award; and my sister, Cynthia, was driving me to the ceremony. My deceased father would have been proud of me. Little did I know that by the time the sun went down on January 10, 1991, my entire life would change.

Cynthia stopped at the intersection. I turned my head to the left and saw a semi-truck coming at us at full speed. It blasted into us, and I will never forget the sound of the screeching tires. I remember thinking, *are you kidding me?* I got out of the car and was screaming. Adrenaline surged through my veins, and almost as quickly, I passed out. The next thing I knew, I was in the ER with a genuinely kind nurse who was checking my body for injuries.

That began my journey with 17 specialists, 735 doctor's appointments, and numerous orthoscopic surgeries. I had broken my jaw, damaged 7 vertebrae and rattled my brain. They wanted to replace my jaw joint with a prosthetic, which I did not want. At that time, I did not know there was another way.

Weeks turned into months. I was not functional. All I felt was the shame of being totally useless. After being released, the only way I could manage was to stay in bed all day in the dark. Friends called my husband and asked him if I was dying. I had a major brain injury – a level 10 concussion, PTSD, on top of the drugs and surgeries. I know what it is like to be a hostage to an illness or an addiction. I developed a staph infection following a spinal tap in a hospital, and it took 10 days to be released and be sent home after having to learn how to self-catheterize to go to the bathroom.

Until recently, I could not even discuss this period of my life without crying. I was using opioids after developing that staph infection, and they wanted to do another surgery. The pain was still there. I finally met another group of doctors in Los Angeles who started non-invasive means of therapy. The doctor asked what I enjoyed doing the most. Without skipping a beat, I said, "Playing my harp." I began playing daily and was surprised at the results. I felt better, and my pain was reduced. I was curious about why it helped. That curiosity led me on an amazing journey of discovery.

I learned that the harp has been used since ancient times as an instrument of healing. Pythagoras (the Father of Mathematics) used it. David, the Shepherd Boy, wrote many of the Psalms in the Bible about why the harp is related to the angels. It is because of the energy. The frequency and the resonance of the harp are unique to any other sound in the universe.

These discoveries inspired me to return to school and move into healthcare ministry. I was hired to start an Integrative Medicine program at Hospice of the Valley. For 25 years, I worked with thousands of patients, families, staff, and volunteers in critical settings, and I saw firsthand how the harp touches the heart and connects to the brain in ways that everyone benefits. It was amazing!

Imagine opioid babies in a neonatal ICU unit that receive an immediate benefit and are released early as a result. Or imagine someone in pain after a severe injury having that pain mitigated not by the push of the morphine button but by the sound of the harp. Or imagine a harp playing at the bedside of terminally ill or end of life patients and feeling the calm and acceptance of the next step of their journey. The hope of one day seeing a doctor prescribe this type of healing is turning into reality.

My personal experience and learning of the spiritual energetic findings, along with my science background, gave me clarity and understanding that brought me to where I am today. The brain knows what to do with the injury for healing to take place, and the harp music helps the brain reorganize itself, from the inside out, to start the healing.

Until recently, we believed it was a "fact" that you were born with a set level of intelligence and number of brain cells that could never be changed. It has since been discovered that your brain has the capacity to change throughout your lifetime due to a property known as neuroplasticity. The brain can continue to form new brain cells via a process known as neurogenesis. Given this ability, most injuries, dysfunctions of the body, and many diseases can heal on their own. Every time you learn a new fact or skill, you change your brain, and your brain reorganizes. Thoughts influence reality.

People can get well without the use of drugs and surgery. At the time of my accident, I found joy, peace, and calm while playing the harp. My brain started working again. It felt like it was being rewired into new neural pathways through the harp. That was 30 years ago.

Every system in our body produces biochemical responses that impact our health and wellbeing. The response depends on our state of mind and how that impacts our feelings and, as a result, our physical wellbeing. If we are in a state of fear, we produce biochemical responses that cause pain and anxiety. Our brain and heart are not coherent. If we are in a state of love, peace, and joy, we produce biochemical responses that allow our brain and heart to get into coherence.

These discoveries represent the passion and fruition of my long journey. I received my Doctorate in Integrating Postmodern

Medicine with Spirituality because of the clinical evidence I discovered about the positive effects of ENERGY medicine. A colleague and I recently published an article in *the International Journal of Engineering and Science* on *Electromagnetic Loop Theory: A New Paradigm in Consciousness Research*. It is a whole new way of looking at consciousness, spirituality, and the need for an alternative to the terrible opioid crisis America is experiencing.

I can tell you, without doubt or hesitation, that you have exactly what you need to deal with whatever happens in your life and create the wellbeing you desire. My core belief is that effective healthcare must encompass both the art of healing and the science of medicine by reducing pain and anxiety, promoting pre and postsurgical healing, opening the door to personal and spiritual growth, and facilitating stress reduction and relaxation.

Thinking back to that traumatic day in January 1991, I no longer remember the accident as the worst experience of my life. It has become one of the best things that ever happened to me – namely, my call to healthcare ministry and the creation of The Therapeutic Harp Foundation.

The Therapeutic Harp Foundation's goal is to document the many case studies that have brought people into a realm of healing and wholeness - from birth to end of life using therapeutic harp music. In 2020, we celebrated our 20th anniversary where we served 195,000 patients in over 30 healthcare settings. The doctors love us and prescribe the harp to help in critical situations!

According to NBC and the Associated Press, Americans spend over $30 billion annually on medicine and medical procedures. People are hungry for new options and for healthier alternatives from the damaging effect of drugs and surgery. My core belief is that effective healthcare must encompass both the art of healing and the science of medicine.

I am delighted to share my personal story and the evidence that I have discovered to clinically prove the spiritual side of healthcare. The energy, resonance, and vibration of the harp connected with my heart and brain in ways that not only soothed me but also promoted physical, emotional, mental, and spiritual healing. It can do this for you as well. It can do this for every person on our beautiful planet. The harp is a wonderful, blissful means to ignite this new Paradigm of Consciousness Healing.

Shame-less

By Kim Davies

I started having intercourse when I was 16. I got into a relation-ship with a boy who was sweet and typical at first. We went to a dance, shared a kiss after a hockey game, and held hands in the hallway. We quickly progressed from this stage because he was tormented by conflicting religious beliefs and hormonal urges, so he pressured me and demanded more.

I was confused and uncertain about what to do, and he started to turn his attentions elsewhere. I became desperate to keep him, offering myself to him in ways that I did not even understand. In a matter of a few short months, I was engaging in oral and penetrative sex. He greedily and guiltily received from me, and I felt almost de-humanized in the process. I went from my first experiences of sensual pleasure and budding sexuality to extreme self-betrayal.

What I was doing felt wrong in every fiber of my being, but I did not know what else to do. I was frantic and felt out of control. I went into shock, and I kept what was happening to myself. I felt certain that divulging my secret to anyone would confirm that I was wicked, stupid, or at least intensely naive. I felt alone with nowhere to turn, and in the act of self-preservation, I disconnected myself from my body and my senses. I abandoned myself during any physical intimacy we shared, no matter how harmless or small.

I survived in the relationship for several more months, veering further and further away from the innocent self I had been. The damage was done; I was broken. I had completely and utterly betrayed myself, and I became consumed by a constant feeling of shame. I continued to experience this disconnection from myself into my 20s. I brought my shame and its effects into other relationships. It was easy to move in and out of physical encounters because I was never truly present.

I was unconscious of the fact that I was literally and figuratively numb. I carried on with an on-and-off relationship with the same boy, whom I now viewed as a villain. It seems I could not break the cycle of betraying myself then feeling ashamed, and at that time, it was all I knew. I felt victimized in our relationship and regularly blamed myself for continuing to stay. Seven years after our doomed beginning, our relationship somehow ran its course, and we agreed to finally call it quits. The final goodbye was utterly unremarkable, and I was stunned.

How did this catastrophe of a relationship calmly end without an explosion? Since I was sure neither one of us would look back, I realized that, somehow, I had always known we were never meant to be. My desperation had kept me with him, but my weariness and defeat let him go. I felt a sort of freedom after that, but little did I know the extent of the damage I had suffered and the ways that shame would rule and ruin my life.

I met my beloved when I was 24. At the time, I was experiencing a massive swell of self-confidence. I had graduated from college, had a full-time job, and was living on my own. I was fierce in the way that I presented myself to the world. I was no longer willing to betray myself to any person, any man, and it showed. My beloved was attracted to my confidence from the start, and we were together from the night we met. We were intimate early in our relationship, and our union was blessed by true love.

We had safety, trust, and genuine admiration for one another. There were moments in the beginning when caught up in the frenzy of this new love, I felt pleasure in my body and enjoyed our sexual relationship. He was affectionate, complimentary, and allowed me the space I needed to be comfortable with our intimacy. We married 2 years after meeting and began our life journey as husband and wife. I had never been happier or felt more whole.

It was a staggering defeat when things began to crumble. Only 1 year in to our marriage, I began to feel the pressure that was so familiar, the pressure around showing up for and being present during sex. He wanted to be in communion with me, and this was terrifying. There was so much at stake, but the effects of the trauma I had experienced when I was younger took over. I hid inside myself during intimate moments and stayed metaphorically quiet, with my eyes squeezed shut, until it was done.

Guilt and shame consumed me once again, and my inability to be intimately open with my husband was like a devastating blow that I delivered repeatedly. For him, it was the ultimate and complete rejection. I saw all the ways that my shame and shutting down hurt him, but I could not find the strength or the courage to do anything different. I was completely stuck.

In the more than 20 years to follow, my husband and I maintained an intimate relationship defined by my inability, and often refusal, to surrender myself to pleasure and to him. We labored and fought; we strategized and tried. We were both committed to our union, but no matter what, the future of our love life was always unclear. There was no assurance that a resolution to our challenge could ever be reached, but we still kept at it.

Many times, I felt defeated and rundown; I believed that I would never break free from the weight of the shame I carried. I could not conceptualize how I would recover and move forward toward healing the trauma of my past. We journeyed on with our dysfunctional dance of him pressuring me and me rejecting him, and it seemed we would never make it to a place where we both were truly happy. Accommodating my shame exhausted both of us, and it cast a dull hue on our otherwise colorful and wonderful life.

It was 22 years into our marriage when I finally gave up. Following another disappointing intimate encounter, where I felt the familiar pressure and relayed the damaging rejection, everything came to a halt. In a hasty split second, I made a decision. I was done. I was SO done.

It was no longer acceptable for us to continue in this manner, and I was no longer willing to hide. This decision was not exactly a conscious one, but something in me shifted, and I was reconciled. I was angry and tired and totally over being controlled by shame. It wasn't that I hadn't wished and worked for this previously, but my soul decided it was finally time.

I believe this was the tipping point because afterward everything changed. I stated, well, shouted, my intention to my husband and started immediately in a new direction. I would not stop until I had rid myself of shame and stepped completely and fully into my relationship with him. Any doubt I had in my ability to make this happen vanished, or it was no longer relevant. I was living an Anais Nin quote that had stayed with me for years, "And the day came when the risk to remain tight in a bud was more painful than the risk it took to blossom." But first, I had to acknowledge my shame and work through the hold it had over me.

The process was in no way, shape, or form easy. There was counseling, crying, meditation, medication, and many, many hours of regret. There was sadness for time lost in our marriage and grief for my sweet younger self. There was anger at being trapped by my trauma, and there was tenderness toward trying my best. There were supportive witnesses to my revealing and words shared with my husband that healed. The process was complex yet natural; the work was profound and so hard.

I faced my shame by finally claiming it. I acknowledged the ways that it shaped my behaviors and affected my marriage. I forgave myself for all the ways I let myself down, and I thanked myself for keeping me safe. I kept moving forward toward the life that I was sure my husband and I both deserved. There were moments of triumph and understanding, and after 5 years, peace finally arrived.

I now show up in my marriage with a willing and open heart. I am fully present to the love of my husband, and I receive his love with delight. I cherish our union every day, and I am profoundly grateful that we ended up where we are. I honor every careful, reckless, painful, healing step that I took on this journey of conquering the mountain of shame I've survived. Through forgiveness and with grace, I have released myself from an inner-prison of my own construction, and I am shame-less and finally free.

Are there still uneasy feelings sometimes? Yes. Are there moments when our old pressure and rejection dance starts up again? Yes. But the difference now is that I see those feelings and dynamics for what they are. *They are ghosts of a past where I no longer live.* Now, I am present and in love with my husband, and our future holds all my desires. Our journey is only beginning; the past is a memory I leave here.

The Power of Letting the Cat Out of the Bag

By Michelle Davis

As I live and breathe, there is one decision in my life that I wish I could change. It is the one decision that I made out of fear and not knowing the truth. It's the reason I desired to create this book in the first place. I wanted to give women a platform to tell their truth so that other women would realize that they are not alone, and fear is a liar.

I barely knew the young man who fathered my first child, and I never saw him again after I aborted it. We had only been dating a few months when I began to feel nauseous on my way to work one morning. I must have pulled over five times to vomit along the side of the road. At the time, I had no idea what was happening; I figured it was the flu or something.

As the days went by, I continued to be sick and extremely fatigued. I could hardly work and even passed out in front of customers, resulting in being fired. I'm quite sure my boss thought I was some young girl who partied all night and couldn't get it together to be a responsible employee. I didn't have the guts to say what was happening; it was clear to me by then that I was pregnant.

I spent several weeks in denial, as I was terrified at the thought of anyone finding out. I felt my only alternative was to get rid of it. I was so ashamed and afraid of rejection that I couldn't even tell my wonderful mother what was happening to me. Not because of how she would feel, I knew she would help me, but it was my father and, subsequently, all of my older siblings that I feared disappointing. My mother would not keep something like this from him.

You see, my father had been married once before. With his first wife, he had 6 children. At that time, I idolized all of them. I am quite a bit younger than they are, but I worked very hard to cultivate our relationships. I wanted them to see me as a sister, not just a kid their dad had with his second wife. As soon as I was old enough to drive, I took myself to their church and volunteered in its youth ministry. I even showered them with gifts at Christmas and tried to be an amazing Auntie to their kids, all to prove I was worthy of their love.

I was certain they would never be able to look at me the same if they learned of my predicament. So, I did what I thought I had to do. I borrowed money from a friend, never telling what for, and made my appointment. I told only one girlfriend, who I knew had an abortion with her mother's help. She drove me to and from my appointment, and I stayed the weekend with her to recover. My mother believed I was spending the weekend camping with my girlfriend's family. I never told my mom the truth.

It wasn't until years later, when I became pregnant again, that I truly realized what I had done. Once again, I had become pregnant out of wedlock; however, this time, it was different. I was in love, and we had already been talking about marriage. My family knew him and liked him a lot. Still, I was ashamed about becoming pregnant without being married, but I decided not to allow myself the same way out. I was going to face it this time, and I can't put into words how devastating it was to see an ultrasound of this baby around the same gestational age I aborted the first one. All these years later, it still hurts.

I told my mother first. She was so elated and supportive. My father, not so much, but my mother said he would get over it, and he did. I had a younger sister living in the house, so she knew. Other than them, I kept the pregnancy hidden from the rest of the family for almost 5 months. My father kept saying that I couldn't keep it hidden forever, but I couldn't bring myself to share my condition.

As luck always has it, fate stepped in, and I remember my father coming into my room, saying that I had a phone call from my oldest brother. It was the day after Thanksgiving. Apparently, at his family's Thanksgiving dinner, as everyone took turns saying what they were grateful for, my niece said she was grateful for my pregnancy. Unbeknownst to me, my younger sister had told my niece in confidence months prior. She was home from college for the holiday and assumed that everyone would have known by then, when she made the statement. She quickly realized that was not the case and begged them all not to say anything.

My brother said they all agreed, and he lasted as long as he could, but he didn't understand why I wasn't telling the rest of the family. He and the other siblings felt close to me, and it hurt them to find out I was keeping something this important from them. So, he called to talk to my dad about it and found out that I was afraid of what they all would think of me. That's when he asked our dad to put me on the phone. That's when I learned some family truths that I didn't know.

My brother and I had an amazing conversation that day. I felt so loved and supported by him; I will never forget it. I still feel an incredible bond with him today. He told me about how his oldest daughter, the niece that let the "cat out of the bag," was born out of wedlock. He had gotten his high school sweetheart pregnant, and they decided to keep the baby and get married. I was in shock at his story; I had no idea. He was surprised that I didn't know, and in addition, he told me none of our siblings would ever judge me because they all loved me.

Weeks later, my older sisters wanted to see me. They took me to lunch and revealed some of their secrets to me. We had never engaged in sisterly conversations like this before, and I loved feeling like I was one of them. It wasn't long before the middle one opened up about having had an abortion, telling me that she was proud of me for not taking that route with this baby. I couldn't believe what I was hearing. I was utterly speechless, but never did reveal what happened to my first pregnancy.

This turn of events was completely overwhelming for me; it was not at all what I had expected. It took a while for me to fully grasp the experience, and even though it was a relief, it was a difficult way to learn a lesson. After almost 30 years, the choice I made to have an abortion still haunts me. I have learned how important it is to be forthcoming with the people in our lives and not make decisions based on assumptions.

Today, I have 4 children. I also have family and friends with whom I am completely honest about my experience. I find comfort in knowing that by sharing my truth with them, they know they are safe to share theirs with me. In addition, I hope that by contributing to this book, I will help other women recognize that they don't have to slay their dragons alone. There is great power in revealing our truths. A special kind of courage is awakened from our vulnerability when we do. A strength we didn't know we had comes alive, unveiling the Heroine within each of us.

From Fear to Forgiveness

By Cindy Farrimond

When I was a little girl in the 60s and 70s, I grew up in a violent household. My dad was a furious man who took his anger out on the people he loved the most, including my mother, my 3 siblings, and me. His outbursts resulted in broken bones, bruises, the taste of blood in my mouth, and fear in my young soul. As the eldest child, I often took the brunt of his anger to protect my mother and siblings.

I was active in the Christian church that the neighbor across the street took me to every Sunday. I always felt safe at a church and prayed for protection often.

Even as a Christian, there were many times that I wished my dad was dead. I begged my mom to leave him. Her response was, "How am I going to make it without an employable skill set?" I would say, "I'll work, mom," and she would reply that I couldn't make enough money to support all 5 of us. I thought *this is my life*, and I had to live with it or leave.

My choice was made clear one particularly difficult night when I talked to my mom about birth control. I was the ripe old age of 17. Although she had promised confidentiality, she had shared this information with my dad when he came home from work. So, at 1:00 am, my dad woke me up and proceeded to beat me while yelling terrible derogatory names such as bitch, slut, and whore. This beating was worse than all the others, and I screamed bloody murder.

When the police came, my dad told them that I was drunk. In 1977, the police took the word of the man of the house and did not investigate. After they left, the beating continued. My mom did something that she had never done before; she intervened. She stood up and confronted my dad.

After the dust settled, I noticed that I was bleeding from every orifice in my body. I had countless bruises, a black eye, and my side was hurting. I later found out that I had a cracked rib. I knew right then and there that I had to leave home while I was still alive. I packed my things while my mom held on to me, begging me not to go. I told her she could put up with the violence; however, I was not going to any longer. My friend's mother took me in and treated me just like one of her girls. I was finally safe.

I never went back home. I married at 17, and by the age of 20, I had a beautiful baby girl. However, after 8 years, my husband left me for another woman. I decided to be a bad girl because where had being a good girl gotten me? During this time, I met my second husband. He was a bartender, alcoholic, and, unknown to me, a drug dealer. I thought I was doing better than my mom, but I ended up with the same type of violent man as my father, only he was also an alcoholic. I felt like I was back at square one.

During this time, my brother passed away at 15 due to a car accident. I was 8-months pregnant with my second daughter, who arrived a month early due to all the stress. After a few months, my husband went on a rampage, and I left with the children.

The next day, my dad summoned me and told me that I had to choose: my parents or my husband. I thought my dad was such a hypocrite. I chose my husband. I thought he was the lesser of the two evils.

My dad forbade me to see my mom and didn't talk to me for 4 years. During that time, I divorced my second husband. I was done with violence for good. I started seeing a counselor to figure out why I made the choices I had. I was on the path of self-discovery. My counselor helped me write a compelling letter to my father. The letter said I missed my family, and I wanted a relationship.

However, it takes 2 people to have a relationship. I asked my dad to let bygones be bygones and for him to meet me halfway. I hand-delivered it. My dad read it, tore it up, then threw it at me and said, "Not good enough." I left once again. By the time I got home, my dad was on the phone, wanting an apology from me for my ex-husband's action. I was not going to give him one, and we continued to argue. This time, I was stronger and did not back down. He said I was raised better than that. I said, "You taught me not to kiss anyone's ass, and I am not going to start with yours," and I hung up. Somehow, those words earned his respect, and my dad was much nicer to me after that.

Some years later, my sister passed away from a drug overdose. With only 2 daughters left on this earth, much to my surprise, my dad started to change. He became kind, funny, and just plain likable. Around that same time, I started taking self-improvement courses through Landmark Forum. I forgave both of my ex-husbands, and I took responsibility for my part in the relationships. However, I still could not bring myself to forgive my dad.

I found Creative Living Fellowship, a spiritual home that was all-inclusive and honored all faith traditions. Their way of viewing spirituality and connection resonated with my soul. I took classes and decided to become a Practitioner (comparable to a Chaplain in other faith traditions). These classes made me take a long hard look at myself and address parts of my past that I needed to clean up. One of those parts was forgiving my father. I learned that forgiving is not condoning an act, and by not forgiving, I was *drinking poison and expecting someone else to die*. I practiced Ho'oponopono, a Hawaiian forgiveness practice of saying, "I am sorry, please forgive me, thank you, I love you."

Over time, with faith and a huge support system, I forgave my dad. We both were making every effort to be better people. I went on to become a Minister. My dad became a father that genuinely cared about his two remaining children.

Shortly before receiving my Ministerial degree, my dad was diagnosed with kidney cancer. Fortunately, he only had cancer in one kidney. When he was in surgery, I prayed for him to live. Afterward, I realized that I had come full circle, from wishing him dead to hoping that he would live. He did indeed live. I've had some good years and great times with my dad, including dancing, long bike rides, going to the movies, lunches, plays, car shows, and, his favorite, going to NASCAR.

Fast forward to the present, my dad is now 80 and has the beginning of Alzheimer's. He has his good days and his bad days. On some of those bad days, I've seen him become that angry man once again. Seeing him that way again is a big trigger for me. I want to run far away, and a tiny part of me thinks he deserves this. *Why should I help?*

When this happens, I refer back to something John Kim said, "We all have issues because we all have stories. And no matter how much work you've done on yourself, we all snap back sometimes. So be easy on you. Growth is a dance, not a light switch."

At this point in my life, I have a mentor to help me set boundaries and stand in power, not fear. Setting boundaries applies to many areas of my life and particularly helps me deal with my dad. I also take classes in the Art of Feminine Presence®. There are practices in this teaching that help me to deal with my father in the most loving way I can, all the while protecting my own heart.

Is this easy? No, but it is worth every effort to know I tried my best to go from fear to forgiveness, and I succeeded.

From Loss to Enlightenment

By Jessica Garcia

As a first-grader, when the end of the day bell would ring, a sting of panic would enter my body, making it difficult to breathe. I would rush home to assist my mother in cleaning up the house. It was in those moments that the worry would set in. I wondered what kind of mood he would be in today. I hoped and prayed that it was one of his good days.

Oh, how his good days, in my eyes, were the best days. I would get to sit on his lap and drive his grey pickup truck to Circle K and indulge in sticky, delicious cherry pies. We would spend a day at Castles and Coasters, where he would build up my courage to go on the big green roller coaster or ride the Magic Carpet until we were purple in the face. We would spend weekends at the Flea Market, where he would spoil me with little unique trinkets, like my very own pink spotted lunch box piggy bank equipped with its own lock and key.

Looking back, those handful of good days are the only happy memories I have of my dad. More often than not, he would be in one of his bad moods. When he was, I would walk in his presence but try not to be seen or heard because I was afraid of irritating him. The smallest of things could set him off, and the biggest of reactions would follow.

During those days, my happy place was my closet. I found a way to shut and lock myself in the white doors from the inside. I would sit in the corner of the dark, musty closet and escape the yelling. I would play with my Cabbage Patch doll, Darlene, and we would transport ourselves to our castle in the mountains, as far away from the hate as we could imagine.

Even when we were together as a family, we were never really together. My dad was absent a lot. When he wasn't at the bar, even when his body was present, his mind was in a fog of alcohol and demons. When my mom and dad told my brother and me that they were going to separate from each other, I had a faint sense of relief. Not fully knowing what that meant, I hoped that it would mean my mom would be less sad, and the yelling would finally stop. I was young and naive.

We moved into a brown two-story townhouse, the most beautiful palace I had ever seen, where I got my very own room and enough space for all of my Barbie Dolls. It seemed like a paradise for my mom, brother, and me. It was a safe space he could not touch. I was too quick to feel a sense of relief because it was in his nature to control, so he moved right around the corner, keeping us within his reach and on the edge of our seats. My brother and I had to spend every other weekend at his apartment, according to the court arrangement, and we always had our rollerblades in our backpacks.

When at my dad's, I would spend countless hours in front of the television, watching my big, purple dinosaur friend Barnie or my afro-haired babysitter, Bob Ross. I wasn't allowed to go outside with my brother and his friends, and I wasn't allowed to go into my dad's room where he and his friends would stay locked up. One day, I had gotten hungry, and I couldn't find anything for myself to eat. I knew better than to bother him, but I knocked anyway.

I knocked on his bedroom door tirelessly until he answered in a cloud of smoke. I caught a quick glimpse of a half-naked woman on the bed, along with drugs and a strong smell of alcohol. In an instant, the door was slammed in my face. I laced up my rollerblades and headed home, where I knew my mom would be with open arms and a plate full of food.

I was the typical little girl who loved to draw and write notes to my mom and dad. As parents do, they would proudly display even the smallest of artwork around the house. Right next to my school photos would sit a crayon drawn picture of the sunset over the mountains with m-shaped birds flying in the sky. The love that went into those pictures was so big, which is why the hurt was equally as big when they would end up on the front lawn of our townhouse in a brown paper grocery bag. This was my dad's way of saying that he didn't want anything to do with us anymore. He would bag up anything and everything that reminded him of us and throw it at our feet like he was taking out the trash.

My mom tried hard to get to the bags before we saw them. She was always doing what she could to protect us. It wasn't until I got older that these memories fully registered. As a young girl, my daddy could do no wrong; I was daddy's little girl. The good days surpassed the bad ones in my mind. And no matter what, he was still my father, and I thought it was my responsibility to make him happy, to make the pain stop.

The pain eventually did stop, by my father's hand when he took his own life. I remember that day so vividly. Dinner time was approaching, and my brother and I were in the living room, playing and watching TV. Suddenly, there was a knock at the door. It was one of my mom's close friends. Another knock came not too long after, and it was my godparents. By this point, I thought we were having a party.

I went to find my mom, to let her know that the party was starting without her. I couldn't find her anywhere. I finally noticed the phone cord trailing into our downstairs half bathroom. As I followed the cord and slid the white sliding door open, all I saw was my mom's puffy red eyes; I heard her raspy voice speaking to someone on the phone and saw a pile of tissues on the floor. The party was over as fast as it had begun.

When she finally emerged, we all sat down in the living room, except my godfather, who was posted by the front door. The next moments are not so clear. I remember my brother running for the door, where he was met with an embrace from my godfather. I was still, silent, and numb.

How do I grieve for someone I didn't really know? Shouldn't I feel a sense of loss instead of a sense of relief? Shouldn't I be crying at his funeral; isn't that what daughters are supposed to do? Shouldn't we be talking about him, living in his memory? I couldn't remember him, and no one else seemed to want to.

I spent the first years after his suicide doing what I thought I was supposed to do; daydreaming that he was a secret agent in the CIA that had to fake his death, talking about him like he was a hero that had left a hole in my heart, or having people feel bad for the poor little girl whose father killed himself.

As the years went by and I got older, I started to try to make sense of what happened scientifically. I went looking for any glimmer of memory that I had not already replayed a million times over. I searched for answers outside of my family, who still clammed up when I would mutter his name. My biggest questions were how he committed suicide and if he was high or drunk when it happened. Maybe, it wasn't intentional. Maybe, he didn't mean to leave his little girl.

I did what any logical girl would do. I called the county public records and asked my questions. The kindest man listened to my stammering and nervous voice; he asked me how old I was, and I explained I was old enough to know what happened to my father, even if my family didn't think I was. He gently persuaded me to tell my mother I had called and, if she still didn't open up to me, to call him back. He opened up the lines of communication between my mother and me, for which I am still grateful.

Over 2 decades later, I know that there are no answers to any question I have that will ever make sense. There will never be an answer to the biggest question I have, the *"Why?"* One thing I can say for certain through all of my healing, investigating, and realizations is that my father did my family and me a justice when he committed suicide; he opened doors to possibilities that would have otherwise been difficult to achieve. This level of enlightenment took a long time to grasp.

I have realized that his lifestyle and control would have steered my family and me into a dangerous direction, but he set us free, just like the birds in one of my landscaped drawings. Along the way, I have found my own answers to this big question. Over the years, I have had friends and family members lose their loved ones, including several fathers. Although each situation is unique, my understanding of their pain has provided comfort and solace. This is my answer to the why.

I have met people in my life who lived through a similar reality and turned to negative outlets to express their feelings. Some people hit their rock bottom and never get back up, using their experiences as an excuse, playing the victim. Without giving it a second thought, I was able to express my feelings through my schooling. I could have ignored the impact my father had on my life because it was for such a short 8 years. Instead, I made my story heard, and along the way, I accomplished my highest dreams, graduating with my Master's Degree from Johns Hopkins University, traveling the world, helping people feel connected along the way, and having a family to call my own.

I don't think of myself as an inspiration to others. I don't believe I found some secret recipe to grief or overcoming the loss of a parent as a child. At the time, I did what I thought was the right thing to do; I tried my hardest to succeed. I didn't always make the right choices. I have made mistakes along the way, but like the loss of my father, I have tried to learn from every experience. Let me tell you what I have learned.

My journey has taught me that you should speak your truth and tell your story. Your truth could assist someone in need. Everything truly happens for a reason. God doesn't give you more than you can handle. The concept of "family" looks different for everyone; your mom can be stronger than 2 parents combined. Depend on others for support; you are not in this alone. Find positive outlets to cope with your feelings. Use your adverse circumstances to inspire others to find their truth. There is something comforting in knowing that someone has gone through a kind of hell that you have and survived. Don't hold negative feelings in your heart.

Starting my own family has made me think of my father more often. I thought of him on my wedding day. I thought of him the day my son was born. I think of him every time my husband and I go visit his father at the cemetery. I think of him fondly. I do not hold any negative feelings toward him, for the things he did when he was alive, or the things he is missing because he took his own life. I think of how proud he is of my mother, brother, and me. I like to imagine his intention of setting us free has come to fruition, and he is thankful that his little princess has achieved all he wanted for her, her happily ever after.

That's Just What I Needed to Hear

By Stacia Harmony

I was 8 years old, and my head and arms were down on my desk in school; all I could hear was indecipherable chattering noise surrounding me. My closed fist with my thumb sticking up was next to my head on the desk; I hoped that someone would come to push my thumb down. "Heads Up, Seven Up" was the game we were playing in third grade. The goal was to guess who pushed your thumb down. No one would push mine down. I peeked to the side to see when the other students would pick their heads up. If I did not, I would be called out individually since I could not hear the teacher say, "Heads Up, Seven Up!" This was one of my earliest memories in which I felt "different" from others.

I was born with a hearing loss of about 35% in both my ears. The more significant percentage of hearing loss is mostly in the area of human communication or speech. I was told it was nerve damage with no determined cause. The type of hearing loss I have is referred to as the "Cookie Bite" loss. On the audiogram, it looks like someone took a "bite" out of the line on the graph (the chart that shows the hearing loss by decibels: high pitch vs. low pitch).

My mother discovered it when I was about 2 years old. I also could not walk, due to my hearing, until I was 2 years old. Again, professionals could not say what the cause of the delayed walking was. That was when all the special treatment began. I had to go to a "special school" to learn to walk. I also had to go to extra doctor's appointments and tons of audiologist appointments. The non-stop audiologist appointments were to test the severity of my hearing loss. I would have to have this gooey, pink putty squeezed into my ears to make the molds for my brand-new analog hearing aids.

In third grade, I truly began to realize the separation my hearing loss had on my life, especially in the social area, which is important for a child's well-being. During this time, other kids would tease me for being "retarded" because I had difficulty understanding their voices. They made me feel left out, different, and as though something was genuinely wrong with me. Some would flick my ears, grab my hearing aids and throw them, and mock the way I spoke.

My spirits were down during this time. I was being pulled out of my class to attend speech therapy as I could not pronounce the letter "R" correctly. I did not mind the speech therapy as the therapist was very sweet and loving with me. My third-grade teacher, Mrs. Brianna, took me under her wing. She nurtured me and loved me. She would take extra time and read with me after class and during breaks. She would talk to the other students about being kind to me. She made a world of difference for me during that challenging time in my life.

I had to wear analog hearing aids, which do not work well with the Cookie Bite hearing loss that I had. In layman's terms, analog hearing aids amplified both the sounds I could not hear and the sounds that I could hear. Therefore, I was getting inundated by extra-loud sounds. I hated them and would take them out at every opportunity. I had constant battles with my mom and teachers about wearing them.

I was constantly in and out of the audiologist's office for adjustments to make them sound "right" for me. Those hearing aids caused me many frustrations. As I moved up in the grades, the school provided me with an "Audio Trainer." Beginning in fifth grade, every morning, I would grab this Audio Trainer. There were 2 devices, 1 for me and 1 for the teacher. The 1 for me had a box with 2 beige-colored wires that went from the box and led to both my ears. I had custom molds made for both my ears. The other device was a box with a wire attached to a microphone that teachers would clip on their shirts so I could hear them clearly.

Again, there's nothing like a huge sign going up to my ears that says, "Hey, everyone, I have a hearing impairment!" I was embarrassed by it because I saw how other students would avoid talking with me. I would purposely "forget" to pick it up most days and struggle through my classes. In my eyes, I would much rather struggle in class than have to bear the cruelty given out by the other kids.

I became more myself in middle school, meaning, that my rebellious streak was showing up, and my shyness was dissolving. I had the opportunity to go to a different middle school from most students from my elementary school. It was my chance to start fresh, to be Stacia, NOT someone who is "retarded" but instead a bright and beautiful girl. It was also at this time when I thought I should start having fun with the Audio Trainer.

I would give 1 part to my best friend at the time. She would take the microphone piece into class with her (we had different classes) and talk to me throughout the class while I listened on my end. Then, we would swap out, and I would take the microphone part and talk to her during my class. We had some fun times, but of course, we were not paying much attention to our studies.

When the teachers discovered that I was not using the Audio Trainer as it should be used, they agreed to allow me not to use it any longer. I still had to wear my hearing aids, per my mom, but

I would immediately take those things out as soon as I arrived at school. Again, I would much rather bear the struggles than deal with other students' indifference toward me. As a result, my grades were slipping. The teachers would talk as they were facing and writing on the chalkboard, so I could not understand most of what they were saying.

I struggled and missed a lot of their instruction. I would turn to the students next to me for guidance. Some would help me, and some would not. It was about this time when my mom sat with the hearing specialist at the school and developed an IEP (Independent Educational Plan). The IEP included some requirements, as follows: All teachers were required to write down the assignments on the board; male teachers had to shave their mustaches to above their lip line to allow me to utilize lip-reading; and all teachers were to make sure they were speaking while facing the class. I also had to sit near the front of the class at all times, which was not my favorite.

Physical Education was one of the most challenging classes for me in elementary and middle school. I thought I got away from the judgment by the middle school students, but I did not. I was always one of the last students picked. I had difficulty understanding when multiple students talked at once during a competitive game. I felt left out, isolated, and unwanted.

My self-esteem was low. I wanted to be included by the other kids. The elementary school would hold Field Day, where I was encouraged to try every activity. In fifth grade, I discovered my running skills in Track and Field. I had joined the relay team and was the fastest runner to run the baton through the finish line. I truly enjoyed that, as it did not involve "hearing" others for me to perform. I carried through with Track and Field until eighth grade when my asthma got the best of me. I had to quit at that time and never picked it back up in high school.

High school was a whole different area of strength for me. I had a great teacher, Mrs. Willow, who took me under her wing and encouraged me to be that strong person I am throughout my high school years. She was a positive ray of sunshine that always had the most powerful teachings for me to learn. As a result of her, I realized that I no longer needed to be concerned about how others thought of me and, instead, do what I wanted to do.

It was time I took care of myself as I was tired of feeling excluded. I took summer school classes to get ahead, which resulted in me graduating a half year earlier with minimal classes during my last semester. I started college classes while others were finishing their final semester of high school. I had friends outside of my school that I would hang out with to fulfill my social needs. I still struggled at times, but they understood that they needed to repeat themselves for me sometimes, and they did it with kindness. High School was a blur of challenges and changes for me, and I am grateful that I had Mrs. Willow there to support me every step of the way.

It was not until adulthood that I learned about digital hearing aids. I got my first pair in my early 20s, and they made a huge difference by increasing the sounds I could not hear without amplifying sounds I could hear. However, with people that I was not comfortable with, I still would not wear them. I couldn't get over the stigma around hearing aids. I believed that if I wore them, then I was "retarded." I was extremely embarrassed by them due to the teasing I experienced as a child.

Sometimes, I had people ask me where I was from due to my "accent." During that time, I would play off on my background of being Lithuanian (which is true). I was too embarrassed to tell others about my hearing impairment. To this day, I get asked that same question; "Where are you from?"

I always dreamed of being a Veterinarian since I was a little girl. I would rescue animals, find their homes, save birds, bury deceased animals, and do everything I could to help animals. I dreamed of having my own Veterinarian office with my name on the building. I have a huge heart for animals. During my early college years, I researched and found a pre-veterinary school in Colorado and applied.

I was so excited to have my dream come to fruition. Being honest and open, I was transparent and informed them of my hearing impairment to ask about their accommodations. A short while later, I received a letter explaining their refusal to accept me as a student as they could not accommodate my hearing disability. My heart was crushed. I did not know what I should do as being a Veterinarian had always been my dream. I felt lost, and I grieved.

I then started on my path of self-discovery. With the guidance of my college career counselor, Ms. Dana, I began taking career exploration classes, personality assessments, skills assessments, etc. The assessments all pointed to becoming a medical doctor. By this time, I had my first child and knew that "doctor life" was not compatible with parenting; therefore, Ms. Dana helped me chose a profession that would be. With her help, I decided to become a Nurse Practitioner.

I went ahead and proceeded with attaining my Associate's degree. During these years, I received accommodations to include a person who took notes during the classes for me. Years later, I applied for the baccalaureate program at a private nursing university. The school officials requested a meeting in which I had to explain the extent of my hearing loss and my drive to become a Registered Nurse. They all concluded that I would be a good candidate student as they saw how I not only work to achieve the requirements but also overachieve and work beyond the minimal requirements.

I had an instructor, Mrs. Bridgett, who had sat one-on-one with me to determine what I could or could not hear with a regular stethoscope. She became my mentor throughout my nursing program. I utilized the accommodations they supplied, and I not only passed the courses but also was also accepted in the Honor Society for exemplary grades. The university even kept a few of my papers and projects as examples for future students. I received many accolades for my outstanding work as I showed the university that I had raised the program's standards. It was a fantastic experience for me, and I am grateful that I had Mrs. Bridgett right by my side, supporting my every achievement.

As a middle-aged woman, I still carried the stigma of hearing aids associated with being "retarded." The term "retarded" was no longer appropriate in these later years. Instead, it was referred to as "mentally disabled," which I was not. Yet, I still held on to that old childhood stigma. As a result of not wearing my hearing aids, I had learned to accommodate by ensuring people looked directly at me when speaking. I would also utilize email for professional communication. When others asked me where I was from due to my "accent," I would still use my Lithuanian background and not divulge my hearing loss.

It was not until I started dating my Other Half that I finally accepted hearing aids as "just another piece of clothing," as he said to me one evening. At that exact moment, the stigma I held for so many years dissolved. He was correct, and that is precisely what I needed to hear!

Now, I wear my hearing aids nearly every day, and when people ask about my "accent," I freely share about my hearing impairment, which leads them to ask further questions. Since one of my passions is American Sign Language (ASL), I openly share that with others. I have been told multiple times in my adult years that I communicate very well, and I am very astute with my conversations. This is one of the many hidden blessings of growing up with a hearing impairment that I learned in my adult years.

Growing up with a hearing impairment was challenging and included many trials and tribulations. However, as an adult, I view my hearing impairment as a blessing. I have learned how to overcome challenges and also have learned exemplary communication and writing skills. I have an incredible level of intelligence and maturity as a result of my hearing impairment. Plus, it has forced me to focus on continued self-improvement.

My best advice to anyone who may be struggling with a life-long disability is to find the blessings within it and learn to appreciate all the lessons you have learned along your path that made you the beautiful person you have become. That is what I have done and how I've become the Heroine of my own story.

*Names have been changed to protect the privacy of individuals.

Stand Tall

By Claudia Hartman

Trauma is an experience that rupture's the sense of self. We lose our understanding of who we are. And so, something remains unfinished within us. There is a lapse in our story.

~ Pumla Gobodo-Madikisela

As I run my fingers along the black and white photograph of my mother embarking on her voyage across the Atlantic to come to America from Germany, I realize my own story begins there. She is clasping her raincoat, looking brave, while at the same time, desiring comfort. She is beautiful and young, facing her unknown future like a pioneer. I imagine her face lighting up as she sees the torch of the Statue of Liberty upon arriving at the shores of New York along with hundreds of other immigrants.

About six months later, my dad emigrated from the Netherlands and followed Henry Hudson to Albany, NY, to start his life as an artist. He also grew up during the war, loved tulips, and said hello like it was a color. Their paths converged when he saw my mother emerge from a lake at an International Club picnic, and it was love at first sight. His dashing looks and persistence eventually won her over, although she was cautious of his artistic temperament.

I was the firstborn girl. We lived on the upper floor of my German grandparents' home while my parents worked to get enough money together for my dad to design and build our first house. During this time, dad was an apprentice to become an architect. Architecture brought together his creative talent for space and design. I often saw him sketch ideas of churches and homes on the back of napkins.

My childhood was a magical time of growing our own food, enjoying the spectacular flower gardens my grandfather planted, and enjoying the frequent gatherings with other immigrant families. Life was filled with music, campfires, and community meals as I danced in the grass and chased fireflies.

My mother wanted to be an actress like Marlene Dietrich and performed in community theaters both in Germany and in the States, along with my grandmother Oma. She was gifted with words even in her non-native tongue and wrote poetry, letters, and articles about things that mattered to her. She cared about many things, such as eating healthy, growing our own food, creativity, and the environment. She knew how to bring beauty to things and was a talented seamstress who made costumes and adorable matching outfits for her young girls. She was way ahead of her time in her ideas and often felt out of sync with the culture and times.

We often performed together as a family like a small version of the Trapp family singers to raise money for various environmental and social causes that my mother believed in. My mom played folk music on the guitar, and we sang harmony. Music, art, and drawing were all critical pieces of my simple yet sweet upbringing.

One summer, we hosted a young black girl from New York City because my mom thought it was important to broaden our views and experiences on race and diversity. We lived in a small town where there weren't many other ethnic groups or races. We were fascinated by how she tended to her hair and made rows in straight lines. There were many excursions to nearby lakes, canoeing, and picnics—the simple summer pleasures combined with giggles and fun that teenagers can have. My mom published an article, with the Fresh Air fund, about our experience and how it changed all of us.

Mom started an environmental group, Save our Surroundings (SOS), to help with tree reclamation in our small town. She opened a gently used children's clothing store, thinking recycling was a smart idea. They were great ideas! However, she was about 25 years ahead of everyone else in her thinking, and as a woman, and many people didn't understand and couldn't appreciate what she was up to.

I did my best to fit in and assimilate into American culture. Still, mom insisted that my sister and I continue to speak German, wear homemade clothing, eat healthy lunches, and restrict our television exposure. She felt it was essential for us to honor our heritage as well as embrace being American. Keeping this balance hindered socializing with others and keeping friends. I remember bringing over some girls to my house after school, and we saw sweetbreads (pig's brain) draining in the sink. I was horrified, as were my friends.

It was hard to keep friends for long because our family was so different from mainstream American culture. This created a lot of emotional pain for my mother, who regularly went through bouts of depression. Mom was already sensitive, and it was painful for her to watch her young girls navigate between staying proud of our heritage and conforming to social norms. It was hard for her to hear how my sister would get teased about "being a Nazi" and physically abused at the bus stop for being German.

We were not wealthy by American standards, but my parents always managed to save enough for us to do some special things like dance or art lessons. Like many immigrant families, they worked hard so that their children could have a better life. I had a curious nature and a quick mind and showed great potential, so my mother plucked me out of public school and enrolled me in a prestigious girl's boarding school in Troy founded by suffragette Emma Willard.

My grandfather had worked there, and I received a Reader's Digest scholarship that paid for my tuition and room and board. So, I left home when I was only 13. It was an expanding time of growing and learning as well as a difficult time for my 2 younger sisters who still lived at home, as my mother dipped into another cycle of depression. This one was more serious than the other times.

Both she and my grandmother were diagnosed with clinical depression, something very common to women after the war. They experienced PTSD and didn't know for almost 3 years whether my grandfather was dead or alive. Back then, the protocol for severe depression was shock therapy and mind-numbing drugs. My mother went through several rounds to overcome her demons of despair and suicidal tendencies. She would come back numbed out and not present.

I was not living at home during this difficult time and shudder to think what my sisters witnessed and had to go through. My middle sister suffered from eating disorders during her teen years, and the youngest turned to alcohol, which has been her life-long demon. One time, I asked my mother what it felt like to be in this depressive state, and she said, "It's like being on the bottom of a dark well and not knowing how to get out."

At the crux of my mother's mental illness was a deep longing to express her creativity and talents in a world that did not seem to understand or appreciate her gifts. As her multiple attempts at launching her ideas (such as the children's resale shop and an environmental advocacy group) failed, she slipped increasingly into despair. She often felt unworthy and lost in an unwell society. And on top of that, I think she felt guilty that she was not fulfilled in only being a housewife and mother. She wanted to express herself more fully so she could make a positive difference.

One summer, when I was 16, I attended a tennis camp on Martha's Vineyard. My parents dropped me off at the bus stop. As I looked back, I could see them standing at opposite ends of the car. I said to my friend, "My mom looks so sad like she isn't going to see me again."

A few nights later, on July 4th, after I went to watch the fireworks over the bay, I had a vivid dream where my mother came to me and asked me to watch over my sisters. Feeling a bit rattled, I told my friend about my dream. That afternoon, as we were leaving to go sailing, I saw my grandmother in a van surrounded by bright white light, and suddenly, everything slowed down. She was there to pick me up and bring me home because my mother had died the night before.

I recall lying in the back of the van, looking at the sunset. I was thinking about my mother dying on July 4th—Independence Day. I knew in that instant that it was not an accident as first believed. It took me almost a year to gain the courage to ask my father about it. My mom's spirit wanted to be free from the pain she experienced in her physical form, even though I knew that her soul was eternal.

My mom's clinical depression and suicide were a major trauma that I had to reconcile and overcome. After her death, I turned inward to cope with the devastating loss. As a child, I expressed my energy outward as a dancer, clown, and performer. But as a teenager, I became increasingly serious and withdrawn, trying my best to understand. My father became worried that I showed tendencies toward depression because I would lock myself in my room for hours and withdraw, but that was just part of being a teenager. The grief from my mother's death caused me to turn inward to seek God, and it was then that I started a lifelong journey to come to grips with her loss from a place of higher understanding.

I often wrote in my journal and found solace in nature. I buried myself in my academic studies to ease the pain and make sense of things. I was mature beyond my years and thwarted at the same time. Boys and dating didn't interest me much at all, and it was easy to ignore this while attending an all-girls school. I hid my crazy curly hair under a hat and was flat-chested like the ballerinas I once idolized.

As a result, I got academic and leadership awards and even got accepted into an Ivy League school. On the surface, I felt proud and accomplished, but that was only a temporary and superficial fix. I thought that gaining more knowledge would help me understand more about the nature of life and death. Also, getting accolades for being a good student provided a focus for my grief. But underneath the surface, I was devastated and alone in a world where I didn't completely belong. Someone once said once, "Grief is love that has no place to land."

For me, my grief fueled my desire to achieve and make a difference because my mother's abrupt death left such a big hole in me. At the core of my drive and ambition was the desire to make sense of my mother's death and define my own emerging female identity. Gloria Steinem once said, "Many of us are living out the unlived lives of our mothers because they were not able to fully become the unique people they were born to be." This especially rang true for me; my mother died when she was only 42, and I resemble her.

I have her long legs, curly hair, and creative spirit that seeks to perform and stand out while at the same time feels at odds with the culture. My mom had a beautiful voice and spirit that often caved in on itself. I recognize that pattern all too well. I wanted to be a ballerina, but I stopped dancing after not getting selected for the NYC Ballet student summer camp. I wanted to hang out with the popular girls at prep school, but we couldn't afford the preppie attire, and I often compared myself. I wanted to be cool, but I was too afraid to rebel. I had this strong pattern of sitting in the crosshairs of unique expression and approval, the rebel and the good girl, and living in the paradox.

What helped me navigate between these two contradictory impulses was growing into my own sense of self-worth and power beyond the conventional choices. I was a late bloomer and did not start dating or even think about marriage until my

30s. But deep within, I felt an urge to connect to something meaningful, beautiful, and true, just like my mother did. It was that curiosity that took me to the West, to explore a new world as she did in that black and white photo taken as she embarked for America.

I left the family nest and carved out a life of sweat and grit. Like the Colorado River carved out the Canyon lands, I had a very circuitous career path with lots of ups and downs, loves and losses. I started and ended several businesses and rode the roller coaster ride of life itself. I fell in love with a handsome New Zealander, who contracted a rare form of cancer and passed away just after be both celebrated our 40th birthdays.

My saving grace was that I was driven toward introspection and connection and started a 25-year journey of inquiry in metaphysics, self-improvement, personal growth, workshops, therapy, and more. There was much self-doubt, comparison, confusion, and lack of esteem before I started following my heart and trusting my inner guidance. I had to lose almost every attachment before I started to hear my inner voice of truth. There are times, even now, when I have to go within and get very still in this loud, confusing world to make sense of it.

After another difficult time in 2010, I found Creative Living Fellowship, a center for Religious Science. This started a deep spiritual study that ultimately led to becoming a Science of Mind Practitioner after 6 years. I was drawn to this spiritual philosophy because it is a fusion of ancient wisdom and practical spiritual tools such as prayer, mediation, visioning, and affirmations that reveal the truth of our core spiritual nature.

This inner journey brought me back to remembering something I knew when I was only 6; I am that I am, namely a glorious, wondrous expression of Spirit itself, born of my mother and father, and here to be the highest version of myself. The teachings of Science of Mind, my life experience, and other influences have helped me deeply reconnect with the truth of my soul and being. It has given me grounding and knowing that nothing in the exterior world could provide.

I know without a doubt that all that has happened to me in my life has brought me to this eternal moment to step out like a beacon. There is a call within to stand tall and shine the light of hope and truth for anyone who is feeling afraid or lost like Lady Liberty did for my mother and thousands of others. I believe one of the bravest things that we can do right now is to offer a hand to someone who is struggling and share some inspiration, so they know they are not alone. By doing this, I honor my mother's legacy. Freedom isn't free; it requires some sacrifice to ensure our liberty.

Complete

By Carleta Mei

At a young age, I learned what addiction was. At around 11 years old, my mother started making bad choices. She moved our family to a small town, where we knew no one. My sister and I started seeing changes in her, but were unsure why these changes were happening. She would not sleep for days, her eating habits were different, and I had to start taking care of my sister and me.

We wanted a different life than what she was showing us. We prayed for the life we had before she started down this path. Sometimes, my mom would forget to come home or forget to feed us a meal. I began to assume her responsibilities for us. This behavior of mine started becoming who I was while my brother would come in and out of the home, often staying gone for long periods of time. As we got older, my brother began joining my mom on her road of addiction while my sister and I went on a path of fighting against it.

Watching my mom go through the changes of addiction was one of the hardest things I've ever had to witness. There would be times that she would be up for days; she became incredibly angry and hateful toward us. It was almost like she had become someone we did not even know. The hatefulness escalated to abuse. At first, it was only verbal, then both verbal and physical, but eventually, it was physical, all physical.

She allowed another family to live with us and gave them the bedroom that my sister and I shared, so we had to sleep on the couches while all our clothes remained in the bedroom. One morning, my sister went into our bedroom to get clothes for school and found drugs and syringes in the room. We decided that she should take them to school and give them to the principal while I stayed home to watch mom.

As my sister was getting ready for school, the couple must have told mom that the drugs were gone because my mom went into a rage, screaming at us. She did not bring up the drugs or syringes, but she yelled things at us. She told us that we were ungrateful brats, and we were disrespectful all the time. Random comments were coming from her, but nothing she said made any sense, especially since we hadn't had an interaction or conversation with her yet that morning.

My sister hurried up, and I distracted my mom, so she could leave for school. I talked back saying, "We get it from you." I made sure that her attention was on me and not my sister. She looked at me with this look in her eyes that I had never seen before. It was like somebody else was inside her.

She ran down the hallway toward me, and I ran to the laundry room and hunched over on the floor to protect myself from what was coming. The next thing I knew, she was lashing out at me, hitting my back. I'm not sure what happened to make her stop, but fortunately, she did. She headed back toward the bedroom area of the house, and I got myself together. Nothing was said between us; she just stopped. I sat down to watch TV.

Moments later, detectives came to the house. As soon as I saw them pull up, I opened the door. I quickly gave them a short version of what happened that morning before I went to get my mom. They talked to her and told her what my sister had taken to school. She acted like she had no clue; like she was shocked that this was happening in her home.

Consequently, the detectives took the couple to jail, and their kids went to foster care. My mom told me that she hoped we were happy with ourselves and that the kids would never see their parents again because we could not mind our own business. Over the years, there would be many more situations regarding my sister and me finding drugs, the violent heated outbursts, and physical abuse towards us.

During my eighth-grade year, I started feeling that if I could just become a mom myself, I could fix all of this. So, I was careless and became pregnant at 14. This, of course, would start another chapter of dysfunctional behavior in my life. I had 2 more children and married their father.

I learned early in the relationship that I had traded one addict for another. If my new husband did not have some form of drug in his system, he would become very abusive, both verbally and emotionally. He would even blame me for his addiction. I had so much hatred in me from what my mother's addiction had done, that I thought fighting him back would make him stop. However, things just became worse.

The most horrifying and embarrassing beating I remember was when he came into my work, punched me in the back of my head, and dragged me outside. He forced me to get into the car and go home. He was angry because I was working an extra hour and did not ask him first. I worked in a restaurant, so a lot of people saw what was happening. This was a turning point for me; the humiliation I felt returning to work was enough for me.

I left him (for the first of many times) and decided that I needed an education, so I got myself into college. I knew it was the only chance I had to give my kids a healthy childhood. During that time, my support system was my sister and her husband. They were both attending college as well, and together, we all tried to make sure the kids never felt alone. We did our best to keep the reality around them as normal and steady as possible.

Even with their help, there would be times I needed to take the kids to work or to class, especially since I wanted to avoid leaving the kids with their dad as much as I could. When they would ask about him, I would tell them that he was in a bad place, and he was working on getting better. Many times, I would allow him to come back home, and we would give our marriage another try. Sometimes, we would have months before he would start his old habits, and other times, it was only a few days. Each time, I gained more confidence in myself, and eventually, I was able to see myself being a single parent completely.

When the decision to leave him for good came, I felt peace. Life finally seemed to be getting better, but truth be told, it wasn't. Deep inside, I was fighting not to become my mom. I could not let go of all that had happened when I was younger. I was living life in fear, overshadowed by disappointment and anxiety. I found it difficult to trust others, always doubting what was said to me. I was always disappointed in myself and had overwhelming feelings that I was not doing the parenting thing right. I constantly experienced a high level of anxiety being around other parents because I felt as if they were always judging me.

One day, I realized something needed to change. The only way my life would get better was if I started forgiving those who had hurt me, and I started with myself. I thought back to my early teen years and the coping mechanisms I used to survive the abusive environment I lived in. A result of all this pain and dysfunction was me saying hurtful things to my mom and expressing myself in ugly ways to other people. There were even times with the kid's dad that I would see him at a low point in his life, and I would push him down even more. There were actions and choices I made to try to give my kids more in life, but I knew that I was not doing it the right way, and forgiving myself for that became my focus.

Although it would take many years before I fully forgave myself for what I needed to do to survive then, the day finally came, and it was one of the best days of my life! Only then did I begin to like myself, to love myself. I made a list of everyone I felt betrayed and hurt by and started forgiving them one by one. Some would take me months, others just days. There are people that I was not able to allow in my life and others I was excited to have back. Learning to love others for who they are, not who I wanted them to be, is what has brought me the most peace.

Today, I am living my best life. I now have young adult kids who continue to make me proud every day. My son has given me a beautiful granddaughter, and she brings me so much joy. This year, I married a man who is able to hear me even when I do not say a word; he sees me in the darkest of the night and loves me without conditions. From him, I've gained two wonderful daughters that bring laughter to my life every day. If I had to describe my life today with just one word, it would be "complete."

Touched by Grace....
Transformed by Faith

By Martha Montour

I have faced more dragons than I can count, slayed many of them, and came out as the Heroine of my life more often than not. The journey, however, was neither smooth nor easy.

I was born in the late 50s and grew up in a traditional household with my adoptive parents and one brother. I had a lot of worry and depression as a child and, looking back, realize it colored the choices I made as an adolescent, a young adult, and throughout my life. Always feeling like I was on the outside, looking in with no sense of belonging, I found myself searching for love in all the wrong ways.

I chose to get married very young, as I had no sense of a career or educational direction. For me, the idea of belonging was the most important thing. I had 2 children about 3 years apart and divorced after only 5 years of marriage. Divorce was the first dragon I would face, and I became the heroine of my life and, of course, for my young children. This resulted in me taking a class in medical terminology, which allowed me to take a job as a Medical Transcriptionist. Eventually, I became a nurse and could financially support my small family.

In my late 30s, I met the love of my life, a physician from Montreal, Canada, who came to work at the clinic where I worked as a nurse. We had a lovely life that included traveling, jogging together, and deep conversations. We bought a home, and eventually, we were married. Sadly, he was diagnosed with Stage 4 cancer, and we ended up having only 13 months as husband and wife, a total of just 8 years together before he transitioned on April 1, 2002.

His illness was a very challenging time of so much anticipatory grief and fear. However, it was also a time of deep intimacy and of feeling very connected to another human being in a way that I had not experienced before and have not experienced since. While it is nothing that I would want to go through again, I can look back now and find the beauty that we experienced during this time as well. I wish I could say that I handled his death beautifully, but alas, I struggled quite a lot.

It was so very difficult to cope with losing him. My suffering was exacerbated and kept fresh because I worked in the same HMO where he had also worked. Even years later, the many reminders kept me from feeling like I could fully move forward without him. Despite the pain, I managed to keep going and do the best that I could. I tried to find contentment in my life despite the lingering mantle of grief.

In 2008, I took a Caribbean cruise that traveled to Belize, among other destinations. It was then that I learned the advantages of being an Ex-patriot. I loved the idea of living in a place that had no memories of my life with my beloved husband and starting a new life of my own. I came home from the cruise ready for such a change, and since I was already unhappy in my career, making the decision to retire early was easy. I sold my house and moved to Belize in March 2010.

The first year was outstanding! It was challenging and stimulating to live such a different life. I had no car and only a bicycle. I took a job as a paid volunteer for the Hopkins Belize Humane Society, and over time, I was able to utilize my nursing skills and work as a Veterinary Technician. I felt useful and also enjoyed the proximity to the beach, where I often rode my bike or walked. It was a life with very little money and fewer conveniences, but I loved having to think outside the box and be a bit scrappy to have what I normally took for granted.

Well, this idyllic life was not without problems. There were robberies and break-ins that frequently happened to my ex-pat friends, and there was unrest between some Belizeans and the ex-pats. I experienced a small robbery after about 18 months. Not much was lost, and I had friends that helped patch the holes, fix the locks, and secure my home and belongings. It was around this time that I began to feel restless and to question the viability of my plan to live in Belize for the long term.

At about the 2-year mark, this feeling of restlessness intensified, and I began to feel I was not living the life that I was meant to be living. I missed my family in Colorado and felt that there was something more for me to be doing with my life. I have a distinct memory of sitting at my office window playing yet another game of computer solitaire. I recall saying aloud, to no one in particular, "Something's got to change," recognizing that my life was not as I wished it to be. Little did I know that within 24 hours, my life as I knew it was going to be forever changed.

The following day, I came home from my job at the Humane Society at about 3:30 pm. I remember wondering why my dog Pepe was not barking as I left my van and approached the door to my house. I put in the key, and as I opened the door, a man came from behind the door with a chemical soaked rag in his hands. He grabbed me around the shoulders and covered my mouth and nose with the rag. I attempted to run but was unable to escape his very strong, wiry hold of me.

I cannot ever fully express the panic I felt as I struggled to breathe and to wrest myself from his grip. I saw my life flashing before my eyes, as I realized he very well may murder me. I have never been more afraid in my life before or since, and I fought mightily to free myself and, at the minimum, to be able to breathe. I was successful in moving his hand enough to draw air through my nostrils, but he threw me to the concrete floor. In his broken English, he yelled, "Show me the money." I tried to tell him that he had already stolen all that I had before I had returned home.

As I lay there, slowly taking in the gravity of what was happening to me and considering what to do next, I "heard" a voice in my mind speak to me as clearly as if I could hear it through my ears. The voice said to me, "Do not fight him. Do what he tells you to do. You may stay alive if you don't fight. I fought him, and I am now dead."

One of my dear friends, Miriam, an ex-pat from France, had been brutally raped and murdered several months before. I was sure at that moment it was she who was communicating with me from Spirit, and I listened to that voice! I will not go into graphic details of the crime. Instead, I will share what I must of the story to show how, on that day, I became a Heroine in my life in a monumental way.

I did not resist him and was led upstairs, where the little bit of pay that I had just gotten that day from work was taken from me. My phone was taken and placed in the freezer, and then, I was raped. I tried a few more times to escape but to no avail. He eventually took me at gunpoint to my van and insisted that I drive him to Belize City, which was a 3-hour drive away. I felt that I had no choice if I wished to stay alive, so I did as I was told.

It was a truly terrifying experience, and it became quite surreal as this person was alternately threatening to murder me and then solicitously asking if I was okay. I just breathed and stayed as quiet as possible. In my mind, I prayed that the nightmare would end, and I would be freed.

When we finally arrived in Belize City, it was 7:30 pm, dark, and the busy streets were teeming with people. Belize City, for the uninitiated, is a very dangerous place to be. There are gangs and murders and many unsavory people all around, and it felt no safer to be with my captor. Eventually, he took his things (a backpack stuffed with MY valuables) and left me in the van. He reminded me that he'd come back to kill me if I told anybody.

I got behind the wheel, and I drove as fast as I could with no idea where I was or how to get to the highway. I eventually found my way, and as I saw the lights of Belize City in my rear-view mirror, I began to feel that perhaps I had made my way to freedom! The panic that I'd been sitting on suddenly bubbled up, and I began to cry hysterically and pray aloud.

I made it to about 1 hour from my home when the van died. I was pushing it toward the shoulder when a car driven by a young American man and his girlfriend stopped and offered me a ride. They were heading right by my home in Sittee River, so they delivered me to my door at about 10:30 pm. They graciously came inside with me as my home had been left open and unlocked for the past 7 hours. My dog had been barricaded, and we released him to both his and my relief.

They left, and I got my phone from the freezer and was grateful it still worked. I began calling all of my friends but could only reach voice mails. I felt quite unsafe as I had no way to lock my home and no vehicle. I finally reached my Belizean friend, and he notified the local police. He arrived on his motorcycle and stayed with me until the police arrived.

I opened my door to four officers. One of the female officers greeted me by saying, "It is your own fault this crime happened; you are white and live here alone." The greeting was obviously very unkind and not at all helpful. And things only went down-hill from there.

They took me in their squad car to the police station, where I gave my statement. In the early morning hours, a friend, for whom I had left a voice mail, called. He came to get me and dropped me off at a dear friend's house, an ex-pat from the UK, who greeted me with open arms and cried with me as I shared my ordeal.

I stayed with her for a few days and then was offered a room at the resort across the road from her. I stayed there for about 12 days at no charge until I secured an apartment on the beach. I never went back to my house to live in. After 2 weeks, a friend took me to get all of my belongings, and that was the last time I went inside. Everything that I still had to do with my home and property, I did from a distance, mostly from the US after my return.

Getting past the PTSD of this crime and the very real threat of being murdered by the perpetrator, who is still at large, is one of the more difficult things I have ever done. I did eventually purchase a vehicle and make arrangements to return home to Colorado to visit my family that June, which was about 3 months away. I knew that would go a long way toward helping me process this very frightening ordeal.

I also took advantage of a healer named Aurora, who lived in the nearby Mayan Village. She did a spiritual healing for me, and she showed me some rituals that gave me a lot of comfort. One that helped me the most was taking a leaf and rubbing it over my body to absorb any negativity then standing at the majestic Sittee River. With my back to the river, I threw the leaf into the water. I then turned and watched it take my negativity and float away. I will always be grateful to Aurora for her kindness and healing offerings.

Soon after, my time to go back to Colorado had come. My plan had been to be in Colorado for only a month. However, once I started to relax a bit, I was able to realize that my time in Belize, and its value to me, had come to an end. It was no longer fun and exciting and instead had become a place of fear and isolation. I extended my stay in Colorado by a month. In that time, I opened myself to the Universe for how I could make my way back simply and safely.

I returned to Belize, but left it for the last time in August 2012 with 3 full suitcases. I sold or gave away everything else and started life anew in an apartment in Colorado. I choose to look back on my time in Belize with gratitude, as I learned to live in a third world country and to live much differently from ever before. I am grateful to have become stronger and more resilient from that experience.

The road to healing has been a long one and not always linear. I availed myself of therapy via a program called RAP. It was a sliding scale counseling program to assist women who had been victims of rape. I spent 5 months in that program and was able to significantly decrease my symptoms of anxiety and depression.

It was wonderful to live near my children again and to be near my beloved mother, who was 85 when I returned. My timing was good as my dear mother's health began to decline, and I had the blessing of spending much meaningful time with her and helping her a lot in her last 2 years of life. In addition, my beloved granddaughter Emily was born in 2014 to my daughter in Phoenix. It will always be a highlight to not only have been present for her birth but also to have the honor of cutting her umbilical cord. It created a bond that is as strong today as the day she arrived. She is one of the very good things in my life.

Over the years, I've developed a lot of spiritual practices and learned to manifest so much good! I've written about 70 essays and published them with a blog writing company, and I plan to create an anthology book using 50 of the best ones. Writing has been a lifesaver and a creative outlet. I again have my own home, a small condo (in Phoenix, where I relocated in 2014), a new car, a dog, and two cats that give me so much love and joy.

I learned to forgive myself for the choices and decisions I made when I didn't know better and to forgive others for the things they have done to me. I've learned to be grateful for it all! In gratitude, we shift the energy, and we find even more that we can be grateful for, too. I wish to spend the remainder of my life writing and sharing and inspiring others to live life to its fullest. I am especially excited to be part of a tribe of strong women who, like me, don their Super Heroine's Cape every so often and do big things in their lives.

I've learned that being a Heroine of my life is not a one and done! It may happen repeatedly, but I now know that I can slay whatever dragon comes my way. Here's to all the strong women. May we know them, may we raise them, may we be them!

In Honor of an Angel

By Cerise Patron

On June 1, 2011, I gave birth to my second child, Mateo. He was born silent and went directly to Heaven.

My pregnancy was unexpected but beautiful and almost entirely healthy and uneventful. I had given birth 3½ years before by cesarean because the doctors were afraid (unnecessarily) that my daughter would be too big to birth naturally. I decided that this time was going to be different. I was going to reclaim my power, give my son the best gift I could give him, and birth him without medications in the most natural way possible.

My husband and I decided the best way to do that would be in Peru, South America. Since that is where my husband was born and raised, we knew we would be surrounded by family. We would find connection and power in ways we could not have here in the US. We also wanted to give my husband's parents the gift of having a grandchild born in Peru.

We took our budding family and moved temporarily to Peru to live in a beautiful apartment overlooking Miraflores. We found an amazing Doctor with 17 years of experience and a doula who would help us through the process. At every checkup, our little boy and I remained healthy. We were so excited to bring him into the world.

At 7:00 am on the morning of June 1, I had been laboring all night at the birthing center attached to the hospital and felt like something was wrong. Our doctor checked Mateo's heartbeat, and all seemed well. I took an hour to walk around and continued progressing labor.

Once I laid back down in the bed, the midwife tried to find his heartbeat again but couldn't. She said the doppler was probably broken, but I could see in her face the fear. My own fears came up, and I began to pray. We went next door to the hospital for an ultrasound, and there my deepest fears were confirmed. We heard the words that will echo forever in my ears. "Your baby doesn't have a heartbeat. He has passed away."

I watched as the doctor, the midwife, the doula, and my husband burst into tears. But I couldn't cry. I know now I was in shock. It was not possible that this was happening to me. I sat in silence as my husband wept. Then, the doctors gave me options. I could continue to give birth naturally, or I could be put to sleep, have a Cesarean, and never have to see him. No mother should ever need to make such a decision, and I knew I could not, at least not until I connected to my tribe.

My in-laws arrived and cried with my husband, but I still shed no tears. I needed to call my family and friends in the United States. I borrowed my father-in-law's cell phone and began calling. I called everyone, one person at a time, from a list in my head. I would always start the conversation the same way, "I have news that I need to share, and I need you to be sitting." I was mothering everyone as I told them the news that our son had died. As they cried, I would hold them in my heart; I felt sorry for their tears.

I stayed strong; I stayed in control of my emotions, and I stayed in shock. I had work to do. I decided that I had to birth him and feel him pass through my body. I had to see him and hold him so that I could see for myself if he was alive or not. I couldn't survive this experience if I didn't birth him this way.

Exactly 12 hours after I last heard his heartbeat, I gave birth to my 10-pound, 6-ounce baby boy. He didn't scream or cry as he was born, and the room went completely silent. They laid him on my chest, and I kissed his beautiful cheeks, somehow warm and cold at the same time. I will remember that forever, the temperature of his cheeks. I counted his perfect fingers and toes and held his little hand in mine. Finally, the first of my tears began to flow as I held in my arms, an angel.

The days and weeks that passed felt surreal, I spoke to family and friends. I wept so many tears that I thought I would dry up. I didn't think I could survive the pain and emptiness. After our son was buried, my in-laws gifted my husband and me with a healing journey to Machu Picchu. We took a little bear that played "Love Lift Us Up Where We Belong" when you pressed on its chest. It was the bear I held each night as I cried myself to sleep.

We went to Cusco and visited the sites as my body was healing, and I searched for a way to heal my heart. We explored the Sacred Valley and ruins from multiple cultures. We visited the salt mines and ancient aqueducts the Inca built. We took the train from Cusco to Aguas Calientes, and Mateo's bear was in the seat next to me the whole trip. We hiked up Machu Picchu and stood on the spot where the Inca built their sacred retreat. There, we had a peaceful picnic with our bear next to the Sacred Condor that the Inca believed would carry the souls of their loved ones to the other side.

And then, we got to the very top of the temple structure at Machu Picchu, and I looked over the edge of the cliff, down at the Sacred Valley and the Urubamba river below. At that moment, I felt an overwhelming desire to jump. I wanted to be with my son, and I wanted the pain to stop. I knew those who loved me would mourn, and I knew they would be heartbroken. I also knew that they would understand, and they would know the pain of trying to live after this great loss had to be overwhelming for me.

As I stood on the mountain, I knew I had a choice. I could choose to leave this earth, or I could choose life. I could choose not to live, or I could choose to know that the pain would ease with time, and the Universe would lead me to others who could support me and hold me up so that I could live. I could choose to let the overwhelming emptiness end here, or I could choose not to give up, no matter how empty I felt. I knew in those moments, I had to choose, and I had to choose wisely.

And so, I took a leap. It was not a leap off the edge, but it was a leap of faith. I chose life.

I see that moment as the day my new existence began. Not the day the pain ended, no. The pain is still there, even these many years later. But that day, I decided to choose hope over the pain. I knew Mateo could never live as a human here, but I still had the choice to live. I decided to build a full life in his honor and not only to survive my existence but also to find a way to thrive. I would live my life out loud, helping as many other people as I could.

I reached out for help from my Spiritual Leader and Advisor; she cried with me on the phone daily for the first couple of months. I could feel her heartbreak with mine as she held me from afar, and I could feel that I was not alone. I don't know, even to this day, if she realizes that she saved my life. I pray she does.

The first thing I did when I returned from our trip to Machu Picchu was to join every online forum I could for mothers who had lost their children. I listened to their stories and cried along with them. I formed friendships, sisterhoods even, that remain still today. These women showed me what true strength is; it's not simply appearing to be strong but learning to thrive in the midst of pain. We often call our group, "The club no one ever wants to join but cannot survive without."

I read so many books about how to overcome loss and poured myself into studying. I went through grief workshops and stayed with the programs, no matter how much pain I was in. I saw the tears as my grief having a voice. I allowed it to pour out of me. My husband attended some of these grief workshops with me, and we also found professional therapists to see individually and privately.

We knew that this was something we couldn't do alone and that stuffing this pain would never allow us to heal. We would sit up at night crying and holding each other. We never let each other go. I know that working together on our pain, grieving together, and keeping communication open kept us connected through the worst pain a marriage can ever endure.

I turned to music as well; being a singer and songwriter, I wrote my feelings into songs. I found writing music for myself and others to be very healing. I wrote Mateo a song a few days after his birth and have written many beautiful memorial songs for others who are grieving the loss of a loved one. I always think of my sweet son as I write them and know he is honored in each lyric and melody.

I ended up writing an online blog of daily letters to Mateo for the first year. It was powerful to share my thoughts online and receive feedback and support from others. Many mothers would reach out to me about their own losses, some that happened decades earlier and were never able to be remembered because the subject was so taboo. I am very grateful that my journey helped to inspire others on their own healing journey.

Over the years, since Mateo was born still, the pain has lessened, and my heart has healed some. My son has never been forgotten, and I honor him in many ways throughout my day to day life. I take chances I would never have thought to take and put myself out into the world more because I know his name and his life will be celebrated when I do.

In the first year after losing Mateo, I had many dreams about him. In those dreams, he would always be with another little boy. I told my Spiritual Advisor about these dreams and that

I thought Mateo was showing me that I would have twins; she thought so as well. Exactly 6 months after Mateo was born and passed, I found out I was pregnant again, and then at 6 weeks, we found out it was twins.

On July 13, 2012, I gave birth to beautiful, healthy twin boys. I believe they are a gift from my son Mateo, and every day, they bring my life hope and continued purpose. While they can never replace him, they show me that his life mattered, that he is always a part of our family, and to never give up hope.

I now travel around the world singing, writing music, and speaking to help others see their innate power and strength. I also lead healing journeys to Peru, so others can experience the healing those sacred places can offer. I know I am where I am and able to do what I do in the world because my little boy lived. His life may have been short, but it was so profound for me.

I can't tell you if there is greater pain in life than losing a child, but for me, there hasn't been. I know I could never have made it without reaching out beyond myself to find support and surrounding myself with a tribe of women who held me up when I felt I couldn't go on. I also know there has been nothing more powerful than making the choice to thrive in this life, in honor and remembrance of my own sweet angel, Mateo.

Where Am I?

By Kathy Peters

So, it's been another one of "those" nights, and my first waking thoughts are (and generally in this order):

- *Where am I?*
- *Who am I with?*
- *Where is my car (and car keys)?*
- *Where are my contact lenses (usually still in my eyes, but not always)?*

These are the questions of a 37-year-old alcoholic who has experienced yet another blackout and is desperately trying to fill in the blanks from remnants of the prior evening.

That morning, over 25 years ago, is where part of my story ends, but where the true beauty of my life began. While I had been a spiritual seeker for most of my life, I had succumbed yet again to "falling asleep" and becoming entrenched in the day to day issues, fears, and anxieties that only alcohol seemed to relieve.

Day after day, I would swear that I would never drink again, only to find an empty wine bottle (or two) as my seemingly only option for relaxing in the evening.

Most nights, I wouldn't consciously go to sleep; passing out became the norm for ending a difficult day. Of course, like any good alcoholic, I was great at hiding my addiction. No one, including close family members, knew the extent of my drinking issues. My pattern was to drink alone at home each evening, and on those occasions when I did join others for Happy Hour or a weekend party, I was careful to monitor my spirited intake; unless, of course, I couldn't.

My excuse for years was that I was raised in an alcoholic home. Both parents were great drinking role models for me, and while that was true, every addict eventually learns that the issue they're dealing with is entirely their own. I may have been predisposed to the disease, but getting myself out of the addictive cycle was something only I could do. To this day, I still remember telling my brother I was an alcoholic and going into treatment. His first response was, "How could you...after everything that we went through as kids?!" Well, I believe as siblings and children of alcoholics, my brother, sister, and I all have addictive personalities; my primary choice happened to be booze.

Blessedly, I had several gifted friends who knew how to "reach me" and helped get me into a treatment facility that began one of my most important life transformations. I not only checked myself in for 30 days to get sober but also followed their recommendations to move across the country and enter a 6-month residential treatment facility in Tampa, Florida. I spent the next 3 years immersed in the 12-Step program of Alcoholics Anonymous (AA), giving everything I had to the program. Everything I did, everywhere I went, and everyone I did it with was somehow connected to AA. As a result of numerous poor alcohol-influenced decisions, I had incurred so much debt that I had to sell my home in Scottsdale, AZ, and was living off the remaining sale proceeds. Oddly enough, while I was barely scraping by financially, my

"Tampa time" included some of the happiest and most profound years of my life.

A dysfunctional relationship (okay, getting sober didn't always mean I got smarter!) led me back to Arizona, and I was finally ready to settle down and put the pieces of my life back together. Having been a previously successful CPA and Chief Financial Officer (CFO) for several large companies (I later learned I was considered a "high functioning" drunk, for whatever that's worth), I had been known as a dedicated, hard-working overachiever, but now, I was tasked with starting over in every possible way.

I needed to find new, non-drinking friends and a place to live and work that would support me, all while attending regular AA meetings and doing everything in my power to remain sober. While my self-confidence in my recovery was strong, my self-confidence around my work abilities was at an all-time low. *Did I have what it took to be successful? Had I really been all that effective in my drinking years, or was that just my mind trying to rationalize my addictive behaviors? Could I be productive and successful while sober?*

Friends and colleagues rallied around me, and I did just that; I started over. I began helping companies with accounting and finance issues, and I gradually realized that I was not charging nearly what I was worth. When my financial self-worth increased, so did the job opportunities. I was offered a position as a CFO, and 3 years later, I was recruited by a much larger organization to become their CFO. I later became involved in this profession's national organization, becoming a Board member, and was eventually asked to join an elite group of 30 CFOs from around the country. *Yes, I actually did have what it took to be successful, and I was still sober!*

During my time of "re-entry," a friend suggested we train together to run a marathon. I'm known for a lot of things but being athletic is definitely not one of them! I was surprised, however, to find the rigorous 6-month training schedule gave my body the physical outlet it needed to help me manage my anxieties, and I was truly ecstatic when I completed the Dublin

Marathon in my goal time of 5 hours. Yes, miracles were continuing to manifest!

Not long after that, I began dating again – oh, what a slippery slope that can be for me! I followed the suggestion of the minister of my New Thought church and decided to attend a spiritual conference of the Association for Global New Thought. The very first night of the conference, I was introduced to Michael, and although we both attended the very same church, it took the perfect timing of that event for us to meet and connect. We were married by that same beautiful minister one year later. Oh, how the Universe conspires to bring us exactly what we need when we need it!

One of my greatest joys in recovery has been the continuation of my spiritual quest and metaphysical studies. A number of years ago, I became a Reiki Master, offering healing sessions to clients during evenings and weekends. I was careful to keep this spiritual part of my life separate from my work life. I was concerned that my mainstream colleagues would think I was too "WooWoo" and lose respect for me, yet this was another part of the old pattern of "hiding my truth" from others. *What would they think of me? What if they don't approve?* On and on it went. I was still one person on the inside yet showing the world a different person on the outside.

When I left my finance job, I realized how much of my ego and identity had been wrapped up in what I did for a living and how important I thought it was that the world saw me as a "successful CFO." The truth was that I had been miserable in my job, but I was too afraid to leave the "safe" confines of a great salary and amazing benefits. After a great deal of help, I was finally able to see that I'm so much more than a CPA or a CFO. Those letters after my name might sound impressive or open doors, but they don't tell anyone who I truly am or what my story is.

I've since been introduced to Marconics, a transformative energy ascension modality that I now offer to clients and teach throughout the Western United States. While I still have financial consulting clients, I know that my true calling is of a spiritual nature. I am dedicated to helping people to raise their energetic vibration for their ascension and assist them in finding their own physical, mental, or emotional healing in whatever form that might take. Yes, my path has been quite circuitous, but it amazes me how our Souls are tenacious in helping us find our way Home so we can return to our mission in this lifetime, despite our "slumbering" or choosing to take detours along the path.

The past 25 plus years have held some extreme highs and lows, but I wouldn't trade my journey with anyone or for anything. Having heard such horrible stories of devastation, loss, and pain from others in the rooms of AA, I'm so blessed that through all of my years of drinking, I was never arrested, didn't cause a horrific accident, or harm anyone physically. I have found a beautiful way of living, not despite being an alcoholic, but because I'm an alcoholic. I have been allowed a Grace in my life that has been beyond my deepest comprehension. And while I sometimes wonder why I've been so blessed, there are other questions I'm no longer asking.

I know where I am, who I'm with, where my car and keys are, and yes, my contact lenses are in my eyes, and I see more clearly than ever before!

Free Bird

By Jeannie Soverns

Dragon slaying isn't easy; it's big and bold, and dragons are noticeable. They breathe fire and roar. I used to see my life as the incredible story of an extra-ordinary girl. There wasn't really much fanfare in my life; I had my struggles, my ups, and downs.

Then in 1997, I was diagnosed with Stage 3 breast cancer at 29½ years old. I was devastated, scared, and understandably dramatic; this was a huge dragon. My husband, who was in the Navy, was out to sea for 6 months, and I had our 4-year-old daughter at home. Once I was diagnosed, the Red Cross flew my husband home, and I was scheduled for surgery on February 14, 1997.

I had bilateral mastectomies with tram flap reconstruction, an intensive 13-hour surgery, and I coded once on the table. I felt a bit ripped off that I didn't see any bright lights or find myself floating above my body. I recovered from surgery, and I started chemo. I lost all my hair, which was slightly more of a vanity issue for me than losing my breasts. Since the reconstruction was done during the mastectomies, I woke up with breast mounds and a flat stomach. I always say be careful what you wish for; you do not want bigger boobs and a flat stomach this way.

I loved to drink; I mean **L O V E D** to drink. Kahlua in my coffee, vodka in my tomato juice, wine or beer throughout the day, margaritas in the evenings, and shots at the bar. When they asked me in my pre-surgery interview to quantify my alcohol consumption, I knew enough to be honest because if your tolerance is high, it takes more to knock you out. They asked, "Do you drink more than 3 drinks?" and I asked, "In an hour? Yes!" And with that answer, I was officially diagnosed as an alcoholic.

My liver was showing the damage of the last decade of drinking, and now that I had a reason to drink, such as breast cancer, there was no stopping me. I received a DUI, but it was dropped to a "wet reckless." I think they felt sorry for me. After all, they pulled over a 5'10" bald woman who had just had chemo that day. I spent that night in jail. The next morning, my sister came and picked me up.

Since alcohol would dehydrate me when I would go to chemo, they would have to rehydrate me before I could take my chemotherapy. My veins weren't working either, so they gave me a port in my arm. During this time, I went through tests at different military bases to qualify for an investigational study. It involved using bone marrow for breast cancer treatment, as they did with Leukemia, along with high dose chemotherapy. I got in, and right after my 30th birthday, I headed to Walter Reed Army Medical center for a 6-week trial. My sister was going with me, and my husband had our daughter at home.

My husband is a good man, an excellent father, and a good friend, but our marriage ended in divorce. I couldn't see past my own face to know that he was on my side.

When we arrived at Walter Reed, we walked into my room, and it had a bubble over the bed. I remember so succinctly the terror I felt and how I was nauseated. I turned to my sister and said, "Holy Fuck, *I am sick*." It was the first time that I really got it, *I mean, really got it*. I had cancer!

The 6-week protocol required removing some of my bone marrow, supercharging it, and then giving it back to me. I had to wear a face mask, so I painted red lips on the outside of it and wore dresses. I didn't want to feel like a patient. I wanted to be normal with my IV pole and bald head.

The high-dose chemo was alcohol-based. The first 5 minutes felt like a good margarita buzz such that I wanted to dance on the tables naked. Then it was awful; I wanted to vomit and did. My lifelong friend, Vicki, was there with me; she held my head and my hand. She was there when I could no longer pretend and just cried and cried. It was horrible, and I truly wanted to die.

I met Mary, who was hilarious and around my mom's age. Mary told me that I never had to feel that way again and that I didn't need to drink. At the time, I thought she was crazy. I was still drinking daily, and if I complained to the doctors or nurses that I had a headache, they would give me Dilaudid, a pretty darn powerful opioid pain medication. As you can imagine, I managed to stay high most of the time. I noticed that even though Mary was going through the same treatment as I was, she was stone-cold sober and was always laughing and happy. She also had so many visitors come to see her.

Mary had Stage 4 metastatic breast cancer; it had spread to her bones, and this treatment was to extend her life. She had way more reasons to drink than me, and yet, she was sober and had been for over 20 years. She talked with me about how I needed a "God I could do business with" and the 12 steps of Alcoholics Anonymous. After my next high-dose chemo, I never wanted to drink again. The smell of the alcohol coming out of my pores made me want to vomit. It was horrendous. My last drink was on July 31, 1997. It was a glass of red wine at an Italian Restaurant in Washington, DC. Had I known it was to be my last drink, I would have had another.

It wasn't only Mary talking to me or the alcohol-based chemo that got me to stop drinking. It was also a spiritual experience that changed the course of my life. I had been praying that I would die after the chemo. I didn't know how I was going to live or if cancer would even let me. I thought of my little girl who I would not see grow up or graduate or have kids of her own. I sat contemplating my life with a cup of coffee and cigarettes (you could still smoke on base then).

I was feeling the warmth of the sun, and I heard Lynyrd Skynyrd's "Free Bird" playing in my head. The line that struck me was, "If I leave here tomorrow, will you still remember me?" I thought about my family and friends and what they would remember of me. I thought about what they would tell my daughter about me. I must admit that this was not a pretty picture; even though I know we all try not to speak ill of the dead, the truth would come out eventually.

I started to weep and pray to this God I could do business with. I wanted to be free, free of cancer, free of alcohol, free of the mess I made of my life. I knew that if only this God would help me, I would be ok. I saw an eagle flying free in my mind's eye; I could see and feel that "Free Bird." And when I opened my eyes, a feather had floated down. To me, that was the answer that I would be free.

I kept that feather in my wallet for at least a decade, and I will stop everything to sing "Free Bird" when it comes on the radio. I have seen my daughter grow into a beautiful woman, and I have my grandsons. I found that God, and I have kept doing business. It has been an interesting road of recovery both from cancer and alcoholism. I continued to search and to be open to new experiences. I have remained sober, one day at a time, and have found such a wonderful spiritual community.

I have had many dragons throughout the last 23 years. These dragons have come in many forms, including financial failures, marriages and divorces, and coming out as gay when I was 35. I have learned to suit up and show up. I have dived deep into my beliefs and thoughts to weed out the toxic patterns that I had willingly participated in for years. With each layer I peeled back, I would discover more. I was encouraged to grow, to change, and to be authentically myself.

After yet another failed long-term relationship, I did some more work, and then I found a spiritual community I could do business with and started taking classes. I was developing friendships with soul-minded people. I met the love of my life, Takoda, and I continued in my spiritual education and became a licensed Religious Science Practitioner. I have encouraged others to seek a God that they can do business with, knowing we are One.

I would love to end on a high note and say I slayed all my dragons; it's a done deal. Boom! But, wait, there's more.

I was traveling along this path and enjoying all aspects of my life. I lost weight by walking 10,000 steps a day. I was hiking and getting ready for our vacation in June to Belize. I wanted to hike the Mayan ruins. My life felt good and balanced.

In early June 2019, I had to go to the Department of Motor Vehicles; I had been running around for work and had already clocked 7,000 steps by noon. It was finally my turn, and when the clerk asked how she could help, I jokingly said I could use a backrub. My left shoulder was killing me. I finished my transaction, and I started to sweat and cry. The clerk asked if I was okay and if I needed medical attention. I laughed and said that I was probably just dehydrated. I finished my transaction, got some water at the water fountain, and got in my car.

"Siri, where's the closest hospital?" I said. Thank goodness it was fewer than 1,000 yards away. I drove to the hospital, which, thankfully, had valet parking. I threw the keys at the guy and asked where the ER was. It was under 30 minutes from the time I walked into the ER until the angioplasty and 2 stents were put into my heart. I had a 99% blockage in my "widow maker" artery, and there had been some damage to the lower part of my heart.

They told me they got it in time, and in a day or 2, I'd be released. Then, I heard, "Oh, and by the way, we saw something on your lung. You will need to follow up on that." I started to cry, maybe because I knew or maybe because I was drugged, but either way, I chose to ignore it for my upcoming vacation. I was still allowed to go to Belize the following week, but I was not allowed to hike. We enjoyed the Caribbean and Lobsterfest.

Once back, I made an appointment with my primary physician, who ordered a scan and a referral to a pulmonologist and a lung biopsy. One of the ways that I handle big deals in life is with humor, which I find to be the best medicine. I was telling people I like to get the most out of my deductible. I tried to stay in good spirits, but there would be times I would get very depressed.

How much time do we get? I'm sure I have more time, but I get complacent; I get caught up in the to-do list, and I forget what is most important. Then, there are these late nights when I can't sleep. I listen to the sleepy breathing of my kitties and my honey, and I know how blessed I am. I'm blessed beyond words that I have a life I didn't even know I wanted. I am loved and supported even when I'm crazy, sad, or fearful.

The biopsy came back, and it was cancer; however, they weren't sure if it was Stage 1 lung cancer or metastatic breast cancer. When I received the call, I ran to the bathroom and cried while I sat on the floor, hugging myself. I gave myself a few minutes to feel that fear, that anger, that sadness. Then I washed my face and went back to work. I can't say I was mindful, but I did the best I could.

My identity as a cancer survivor was being challenged after 22 years of being cancer-free. There was a roller coaster of fear and faith that ensued from a heart attack in June, a Stage 4 diagnosis in October 2019, a weekend of the bowel obstruction in December 2019, the COVID-19 pandemic in March 2020, and a fall in April 2020. I really felt that the "God I could do business with" was slowing me down for a reason yet to be revealed.

I had another scan, and they saw 2 more spots in the same lung on the lower lobe. I was devastated; I thought the first scan would be a freebie you know, nothing out of the ordinary. It threw me into a thinking-of-death spiral. The pandemic stopped me from focusing on dying as something only happening to me; With the whole world facing the same issues, I was no longer afraid, and I stopped seeing myself as dying.

I was rescanned 3 months later, and those 2 spots had disappeared. I celebrated. I went from being afraid to finding the help that I needed. In the year since diagnosis, what has become clear is that my life is the incredible journey of an extra-ordinary girl. There is nothing I lack or need. There is no need for a Knight in Shining armor to save me; I am the Knight. There is only One, and in knowing the Unity of All, I am free to love, laugh, and live.

Wayne Dyer said, "Don't die with your music still in you." My "music" is a spiritual class I created called **Humor, Hugs, Hope, and Hummus.** I wanted to remind others (and myself) how enriching humor is in our lives, how human touch (hugs) is healing and cathartic, and that, no matter what statistics, diagnosis, or prognosis comes your way, there is always hope because we are not alone in this world. But mostly, I wanted you to know that there is always room for hummus.

Two Fathers, But No Dad

By Michele Whittington

Michael's Story

Michael Ferrara and Georgia Ashley were deeply, passionately in love. Even though he was many years her senior and, in fact, had a daughter from a previous marriage just a few years younger than she, it didn't matter. They were meant for each other, so they wed in 1942. Their life together was perfect. Well, almost perfect. They wanted to have a family of their own, but that didn't happen. For 10 years, they tried to conceive to no avail. It was so very disappointing to them, but their love for each other never dimmed, and they decided, perhaps, having children was not meant to be. They could still be happy in the life they created together. Then, in January 1952, a miracle happened; Georgia became pregnant. To say they were ecstatic would be a severe understatement. They were over-the-moon thrilled and immediately started making plans for my arrival.

From the moment of my conception, my mother knew I would be a girl. In fact, she joked that if she delivered a boy, she would send him back, which I am not sure was actually a joke. Having a girl was the ONLY possibility for her. And she was clear from the beginning that I would be named Michele, after my father, and it would be spelled the "proper" Italian way, not the Americanized way of Michelle. What my mother failed to realize is that Michele in Italian is actually a man's name, not a woman's, but I digress from Michael's Story.

My parents lived in New York City, and Michael was a hairdresser. Once they learned my mom was pregnant, they decided New York was no place to start a family, and since my father could work anywhere, they left the high life of the city and moved to Tampa, Florida. They set up house, and my father began to rebuild his business. They happily awaited my arrival. On October 18, 1952, I arrived with little fanfare; Mom said she had 2 labor pains, and I was out! What a joyous time it was for us, so I've been told. They both doted on me. Mom got her girl as planned, and my father had another daughter, whom he adored.

One morning, my mother kissed him goodbye for work and was busily cleaning up the breakfast dishes while I slept soundly in my crib in my room. Suddenly, she heard a voice coming from the direction of my room. Panicked, she flew, her hands still in rubber gloves, into my room ready to attack whoever was there only to find that, unbeknownst to her, my father had come back in the house, had lifted me out of my crib, and was holding me and cooing to me. She quietly backed away, trying not to interrupt that precious moment between a father and his beloved infant daughter.

The next 2½ months were idyllic as my happy little family bonded and found their routine. Our first Christmas came and went, and New Year's approached. A friend from New York came to visit, and on New Year's Eve, they had a quiet dinner out and were home asleep by 10:00 pm.

Sometime in the middle of the night, my mother awoke to a startling sound. At first, she didn't know what it was, and then, much to her horror, she realized it was her husband gasping for air. She immediately summoned an ambulance, and from that moment until the day she died 50 years later, the sound of an ambulance caused her body to shudder and a pall would come over her. You see, the ambulance arrived and took my father to the hospital, but it was too late. He had already died of a massive heart attack. At 10 weeks old, I lost my dad.

Sam's Story

Sam Swerdlow and Georgia Ferrara were not deeply, passionately in love and most likely were not meant for each other. Nonetheless, in the spring of 1954, they wed. For my mother, it was a marriage of convenience; a marriage to ensure that she and her 1-year-old daughter were financially taken care of and secure. She would say to me years later that she was "fond" of him when they married, and he always did provide for us. She had to give him that. But there never was a moment of genuine love from her to him. For Sam, it's told that he actually was in love, just not with her. Rather, he was in love with me.

Sam and my mom met in Phoenix, Arizona, where mom and I moved 6 months or so after I was born. Her brother and his family lived in Phoenix, and mom came for a visit. Still grieving over my father's death, from which she never truly recovered, she thought being with her beloved brother, sister-in-law, and their 2 children might be good for both of us.

They lived in downtown Phoenix, and one day, she took me for a walk in the stroller. She walked past a strip center that housed a rental furniture store. Two men were sitting in front of the store talking. As mom walked by, one of the men spoke to her and admired the cute baby in the stroller. Yes, it's true; I was a cute baby.

Taking me for a walk in the stroller along that same path became a daily event, and more often than not, the same man was sitting outside in front of the store. Apparently, business wasn't exactly booming. That man was the owner of the store – Sam Swerdlow. It now became routine that she would stop and chat with him, and he would spend just as much time talking to me as he did to her.

My mom's mom was terminally ill in Kentucky, so my mom and I flew to her home to be with her. We stayed there several months until she passed away. During those months, she and Sam continued to communicate, and by the time we returned to Phoenix, they had decided to wed.

But they did more than wed. He told her that he didn't want to be viewed as a stepfather and wanted me to know him as my father. He convinced my mother and her entire family never to tell me that he was not my biological father. My birth certificate was changed to reflect his last name, and they backdated the year of their marriage to allow for the birth of "their daughter." Michael was pushed into the background, never intended to be resurrected. Michele Ferrara was now Michele Swerdlow.

The sad thing is that, despite Sam's apparent love for me, I never felt loved by him nor did I have a daughterly bond with him. In fact, I could never even call him "dad." From the day I called him anything, it was Sam. Always and forever, Sam. I would often wonder why I didn't feel anything for him. It made no sense to me (because, remember, as far as I knew, he was my biological father), but I felt nothing, no bond to him. He made some futile attempts to relate to me, but because mom and his relationship only grew more distant as the years rolled by, he emotionally and often physically removed himself from the family. They had a child together, my sister, who is 3 years younger than I am, and she was very damaged by her relationship with him, but that is her story to tell, not mine.

There was a cold war in our home, and I seemed to be the go-between. Mom didn't talk to Sam, but she talked to me about him. Sam hardly talked to anyone, but if he did, it was mostly to me, sometimes to have me relay information to mom. And my sister and I, who had challenges with both our parents, often talked to each other about them. If that all sounds very dysfunctional, it was! There was no open, honest communication in our household. It was so bad that after my sister and I both moved out of the house, Sam came to me and asked me to tell my mom that he wanted a divorce. I was co-dependent enough to do it! Their relationship was finally officially over; all the while, I still believed he was my father. Regardless, he most certainly was never my dad.

My Story

Georgia and Sam were divorced, I was 21 years old and living in my own apartment, and my sister was away at college in California. She came home for Christmas break and stayed with mom. One early afternoon, while mom was off at a volunteer job, my sister got the mail and started opening the obvious Christmas cards.

Among them was a card from Rose. Now, Rose was a "friend" of mom's from New York. Rose and mom had corresponded ever since I could remember, and Rose always sent birthday and Christmas gifts to my sister and me. The strange thing was that mine were always noticeably nicer than my sister's. When I questioned mom about that, she would always say it was because I was older and, therefore, more responsible, so I could handle nicer things. But that continued even as we matured, and the 3 years between us made less and less of a difference. That was always a puzzler to me. That afternoon the puzzle was solved.

My phone rang, and my sister was on the other end. Through her tears, I heard her sob, "I don't think we are really sisters. Get over to mom's right away." I couldn't imagine what she was talking about, but I dropped what I was doing and raced to mom's house.

When I walked in, she handed me a letter that was in Rose's Christmas card. A paragraph in it read, "It is so very interesting that Michele loves Italian food. Have you ever told her that she is half Italian?" *Wait? What? Half Italian? My father is Jewish; my mother is English. How could I be half Italian?*

Have you ever had a moment when things that never quite made sense all fell into place, and a light bulb went off in your mind? That light bulb moment could be followed by angst, upset, anger, and a myriad of painful emotions because of the time wasted in uncertainty or the struggles you went through because of the situation, or it could be followed by peace and calm because, finally, there were answers. Finally, there was clarity. For me, it was the latter.

I instantly knew who my "real" father was. He was a handsome, dark-haired Italian man whose pictures were tucked away in a drawer in my mother's room. Whenever questioned about them, her answer was that he was just an old boyfriend. And then, in a flash, I saw in my mind's eye a photograph taken of me in my grandmother's living room when mom and I went to be with her before she passed. On the end table behind me was a framed photo of that same man. How could I have possibly seen that photo a million times and NOT noticed and questioned why a framed picture of my mother's "old boyfriend" would be at grandma's house!?

And who was Rose, you might be wondering? She was my father's sister, an aunt I never knew. The mystery of why I got better gifts was explained. To Rose, I was blood; my sister was not.

So, if this man was my birth father, then Sam could not be. That could explain why I never had daughterly feelings toward him. He was not around when I was an infant! He did not have the special bond that was created between Michael and me, starting with my conception and, perhaps, even before. While I now knew who my biological father was, what I didn't know was why all the mystery and secrecy around it. *Why was I never told about him?* That was something I had to get to the bottom of.

When mom got home, my sister and I confronted her, and as she tried to deny what we were saying and brush the letter away, her face began to turn ashen, her hands began to shake, and tears filled her eyes. She could not deny what was written in black and white in front of her, so she sat down, looked deeply into my eyes, and said, "I've told you I was in love, truly in love, once. It was with your father."

She proceeded to tell us of their 10 years together before I was born, their joy upon my arrival, how I was named after him, his tragic death when I was 10 weeks old, and her decision to marry Sam and keep the identity of my birth father from me so that he could be my father. She was concerned at the way I would handle this mind-blowing news, but all I felt was relief. Many puzzle pieces fell into place.

While I felt relief at the time that I learned this news, it took years and a good therapist for me to realize that this experience was a huge dragon in my life that must be slain in order to become the Heroine of my own love story. You see, my attitude toward men and relationships was extremely tainted. This was not only because of my mother's deep and profound grief that lived with her constantly, which I never understood but always felt, but also because of the cold and distant relationship she and Sam had. Theirs was the only relationship model I had, and it wasn't good. Mom rarely had anything nice to say about him, and she extended her distaste of him to all men. At the same time, she let me know that as a woman, I really needed a man and that a man's attention and affection were what made a woman fulfilled. But then, again, he would eventually leave me sad, broken, and alone. Her mixed messages could not have been more confusing. Add to that my having no healthy male role model – no real and true dad – and I was a hot mess in the relationship department.

It was through a fervent spiritual quest while working with a gifted and spiritually-oriented therapist combined with my own deep desire to get to the bottom of why I couldn't make a relationship work to save my life that I finally saw the damage this secret had done to me. With my therapist's help, I healed the grief of never knowing (and for 21 years not even knowing about) Michael Ferrara, and I came to feel the profound love he had for me even if our time together was brief. It took longer, but I came to forgive Sam for being such a distant, uninvolved father as well as myself for never caring about him and never giving him a chance.

With all of this – and it took years and was not always easy, but I persevered -- I came out the other side. The dragon of having two fathers but no real dad was finally slain, and I began to live as the Heroine of my life. As that Heroine, I wrote the most magnificent love story with my hero, Lonnie, that lasted almost 30 years. How blessed I was to have slain that dragon, so I could create my life with him.

And when that life was over with his passing in 2018, I faced an entirely new dragon. The same dragon of profound loss and grief my mother had faced decades earlier. But, I had a strong level of emotional maturity that she did not have, a solid spiritual grounding on which she did not stand, and the support of the most amazing tribe of women anyone could ever ask for, which was a foreign concept to my mother. With all of that, I was able to slay even that dragon and begin another volume of my life as my own Heroine.

How that volume of my life unfolds is yet to be determined. But this I know; there is no dragon I (and you!) cannot slay. And there are many people to stand with us as we do. We only need to look around to see them.

It is my deepest desire that you have seen many of them in the stories in this book. May they all help you know that you never need to slay your dragons alone.

Your Heroine's Tale

Now it's your turn to write your own Heroine's Tale. And when you do, please send it to us. We would love to receive it! Send it to Michelle (coachingwithmd@gmail.com) and Michele (michele@unleashyourlife.us). Who knows? It may appear in our next volume of "Heroine Tales."

_____
_____
_____
_____
_____
_____
_____
_____
_____
_____
_____
_____
_____
_____

Biographies

Carla B. ~ This is Carla's first time writing a story for publication. She deeply believes in this work and is knowing that someone will be inspired and will experience love more fully because of it. Carla continues on her journey, working as a corporate trainer, entrepreneur, and meditation guide. Most importantly, she shares life (laughs and tears) with her loving and vibrant tribe, including her two daughters (Shelby and Emily) in Phoenix, Arizona. Daily, Carla chants the phrase, "Sat Nam," which is Sanskrit for Truth (Light) is my Essence.

Tara Brown, R.Sc.P. ⁓ Tara is the foremost authority on consciousness architecture, the deliberate designer of great lives. A lifelong student of art, science, and spirituality, she provides eye-opening and insightful guidance. She makes the complex easy to understand. As an Ivy-League trained architect, she learned the systems and patterns for how buildings are created. Studying spiritual principles, she realized that everything in life is created the same way. You'd probably think a person is off  track if they told you that just because no one has built a building on a given city block, you can't ever put a building there. Your dreams are no different. She specializes in helping successful, heart-centered individuals build their dreams, accelerate their results, and create richer, more fulfilling lives. She's been doing this for more than a decade. She loves studying, teaching, and sharing the transformational success principles that she's learned and developed.

 **Rev. Joyce Blair Buekers, D.D.** ⁓ Joyce is the founder of the Therapeutic Harp Foundation, which has been serving thousands of patients, families, staff, and volunteers for over twenty years. In her previous life, she was a successful marketing executive with the IBM Corporation. Following a tragic accident, Joyce moved into healthcare ministry to serve as the Integrative Therapies Director at Hospice of the Valley. After serving as a Chaplain in the 2002 Winter Olympics

and delivering the power of live therapeutic harp in a full range of healthcare settings, she is now a published author, teacher, and sought-after speaker pioneering in the clinical field of Science and Spirituality. The article "Electromagnetic Loop Theory-A New Paradigm in Consciousness Research" (IJES-June 2020) presents a conceptual basis for a paradigm shift in looking at how the brain works through consciousness, electromagnetic fields, and neuronal networks. She is a contributing author to a best-selling book *Love Meets Life-Stories of love... Showing up in Unexpected Ways* (2020).

Michelle Davis, B.S.Ed., M.B.A., R.Sc.P. - Michelle is a coaching professional, educator, and speaker for both personal and entrepreneurial development. Her belief that each person has inside of them all they need to bring about the life or business they want to create is what coaching is about for her. Whether personal growth, success in business, ultimate fitness, conquering fears, success in relationships, etc., she helps clients get from where they are to where they want to be. Her approach is unique, as she relies on a bachelors in education, an MBA, a spiritual life coach/practitioner of Religious Science credential, plus the experiences she's gained from the usual ups and downs of life, opportunities to work with people of all ages, owning several businesses, and parenting 4 children. When Michelle isn't coaching in some capacity, she enjoys being a mother, spending time with her significant other, boating, traveling, writing books, writing/performing music, and working on her soon-to-be-released "Decide Already!" Podcast.

Kimberly S. Davies, M.A.Ed. ~ Raised as the oldest of three children to a Navy couple, Kim grew up along the west coast and in Colorado. She began her mentoring/teaching career after finishing her Undergraduate Sociology Degree at the University of Colorado, Colorado Springs. She was hooked and became a certified Special Educator after completing her Master's Degree at University of Northern

Colorado in 1993. Kim met the love of her life, Jeff, on a fateful St. Patrick's Day weekend in 1991. It was obvious to both that their life story was starting Chapter 1. 29 years, several moves with the Air Force, two beautiful children (Rachel and Jackson) and two loyal dogs (Harley and Radar) later, they settled in Yorktown, Virginia. Kim's passion for teaching children continues today at the high school level. She is a certified Mindfulness instructor and continues her own lifelong effort to empower and love women. She practices meditation, yoga, and personal and mental fitness.

Rev. Cindy Farrimond ~ Cindy is a devoted mother, grandmother, and Religious Science Minister in Phoenix, Arizona. She served on the Board of the Arizona Interfaith Council and the Board of Ecclesiastics at Creative Living Fellowship (CLF). She also served as the Congregant Care Minister for four years at CLF. She has been a Spiritual Life Coach for the past 14 years. Prior to ministry, she was employed by Blue Cross and Blue Shield for 31 years. She enjoys writing, coaching, and spending time with her family and friends.

Jessica Garcia, B.S.W., M.Ed. ~ Jessica is a successful elementary school teacher in Denver, Colorado. She is a proud new mother to a little boy, a patient stepmother of two, a loving wife, a courageous daughter, and a supportive sister. Jessica has spent the majority of her adult life as a learner, continuing to grow her knowledge of educational theories and child development. She was born in Phoenix, Arizona, where she pursued a career in Social Work. This tough work led her to become a teacher, where she felt she could make a positive impact in the lives of the future. She loves to spend time in nature, forest bathing in her hammock, and cuddling up on the couch with the loves of her life.

Stacia Harmony R.N., B.S.N. ~ Stacia (pronounced as STAY-sha) is a successful Bachelor-Level Registered Nurse who enjoys reading and educating others about life experiences. She was born and raised near Chicago, Illinois, and moved to Phoenix, Arizona, as a teenager. She has three amazing school-aged sons. Her

years of reading self-help books prepared her to begin writing about her own life experiences. She also has a knack for computers as she built her first computer, with her stepfather's help, when she was 12 years old. She carried this natural talent into her nursing career. She is working on her Masters of Science in Nursing in Informatics. When she is not reading or studying, she enjoys spending time with her other half, their children and pets, and listening to good music. Stacia is an intuitively wise woman, and her goal in life is to use her experiences, education, and wisdom to empower others to live their best lives possible.

Claudia Hartman, R.Sc.P. ~ Claudia is a serial entrepreneur, community advocate and leader, award-winning marketer, and professional team and business coach and consultant. Her passions include conscious community, personal transformation, cooking, writing, and traveling. As an entrepreneur, she started several successful businesses including, SKY Marketing, Vesta Community Concepts, and Mentor for Higher. Mentor for Higher provides direction and support for people or businesses seeking to elevate their marketing impact, business, and life. She moved to Prescott in 2018 to live in a cohousing community to experience it first hand and start writing a book on why community is so critical during this time. She lives there with her sweet dog, Cooper, and serves as the community chef when she's not consulting or coaching with others or out walking in nature or playing tennis with her partner.

Carleta Mei ~ Carleta has a variety of educational backgrounds, from an accounting degree to licenses in many different parts of the beauty industry. She has always enjoyed learning new things; however, the beauty industry is what she enjoys doing the most. Offering a ser-

vice to someone that will help them feel better about themselves is extremely rewarding to her. In Carleta's free time, she loves being with her family and friends. Anything from a day at the lake to a large BBQ at the park, being around the ones she loves the most is her happy place.

Martha Montour ~ Martha first got the writing bug at age nine by writing stories for the fourth grade, and her mother encouraged her to write. She is the proud mother of a grown son and daughter and a six-year-old granddaughter. Martha was a nurse for about 30 years. She has been writing essays for the past 4 years and has published 69 of them that she plans to use to create an anthology book. When not writing, Martha enjoys power walking, yoga, meditation, and mindfulness.

Cerise Patron ~ Cerise is an internationally recognized inspirational singer, songwriter, motivational speaker, and spiritual tour operator. She has produced 4 CDs of her music and is a for-hire songwriter for churches, organizations, companies, retreats, and individuals who desire a deeper inspiration to help them reach the next level of their dreams. Having a familial connection to Peru, she organizes,  sings, and guides 12-day Peruvian Spiritual Immersive Healing Retreats. She also lends her voice to guided Virtual Reality Tours of Machu Picchu and other sacred and beautiful sites in private, one-on-one sessions. She is a wife and mother to 3 earthly children, and she travels and speaks about her experience with giving birth to her stillborn son in 2011 and how she learned to live out loud in honor of him. Her desire is to spread love and empowerment to everyone she meets, as long as she continues to have breath.

 **Kathy Peters, C.P.A.** ~ Kathy began her career as a CPA with the international accounting firm of Arthur Andersen and continued her profession as a CFO and consultant for numerous private companies. Kathy has always held deeply spiritual beliefs and studied metaphysical topics her entire life. While still involved in the corporate world of work, she became a Reiki Master and was a successful healer for many years until becoming involved in Marconics, a transformative ascension energy,

in which she is currently a certified teacher and practitioner. Kathy grew up in Arizona and has been married to Michael for 19 years. She has two children, four grandchildren, and enjoys spending her downtime traveling, hiking, gardening, and playing with her other "kids" of a furry nature.

Jeannie Soverns, R.Sc.P. ~ Jeannie is a native Philadelphian who loves the wonder of front stoop conversations, playing stick ball, and knowing the Robinsons always had candy apples at Halloween. She moved to Phoenix in 2006 and fell in love with the beauty of the desert, especially after a rain, and the majestic diversity of Arizona. Jeannie sees her life as an open, spontaneous, engaging adventure and has dipped her toes into many different arenas to experience that, such as travel, standup comedy, theater, cake artistry, spiritual life coaching, and even sky diving! Jeannie believes in her mission to give space, hugs, comfort, and encouragement to those who wish to experience their highest and best selves.

Rev. Michele Whittington, D.D. ~ As an ordained Religious Science minister, Michele served a church community for 22 years and is now also a licensed *Art of Feminine Presence®* master teacher as well as a certified Real Love coach. She is the author of *From Our Hearts to Yours: Stories and lessons on conscious*

loving, conscious dying and conscious living (2020). As the founder of Unleash Your Life Consulting, she offers one-on-one mentoring and classes to empower those who want to take their feet off the brakes and fully embrace their dreams. She is passionate about living her life to the fullest and takes the greatest delight in adventures above and below the surface of the ocean, in her tribe of soul sisters, and with her fur baby named Curly.

Index Topics

Made in the USA
Middletown, DE
02 February 2021